WISDOM ON THE WAY

A Mentor's Guide to Navigating Overwhelming
Transitions, Crisis of Confidence,
and Life's Milestone Moments

RUSSELL VERHEY

Published by: Wisdom Way

Colorado Springs, Colorado

www.theadvance.net

Cover design: Double Studios #optimalgraphics

Cover illustration: Russell Verhey © 2025. Mt. Wetterhorn, Uncompahgre Wilderness CO

Interior layout: Naya Lizardo @nlbooks

ISBN-13 (hardcover): 979-8-9916474-3-4

ISBN-13 (softcover): 979-8-9916474-2-7

First Printing, 2025

Printed in the United States of America

I will guide you in the way of wisdom and lead you along the straight path.

Proverbs 4:10

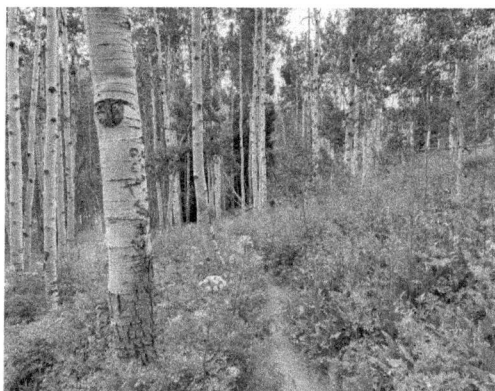

Dedication

Bill Regehr - my father-n-law, friend, and faithful model of a life in pursuit of wisdom. Thank you for 30 plus years over 1000+ cups of coffee, quiet conversations, and encouragement beyond the trials of the day towards wisdom on the way.

Foreword

I'm so excited and grateful that my friend Russell has tackled the big topic of wisdom. In our current age of information overload and endless opinions, the pursuit of true wisdom has never been more critical or more challenging. What makes this book so special is that humility is the key to unlocking wisdom, as God's Word teaches.

Wisdom on the Way isn't merely human philosophy or self-help advice—it's a biblical foundation that transforms how we understand and apply wisdom in our daily lives. Russell has indeed approached this topic with a humble heart and a teachable spirit, and that authenticity permeates every page. Rather than positioning himself as the expert dispensing knowledge from on high, he writes as a fellow traveler on the journey toward wisdom, sharing both his discoveries and his struggles with refreshing honesty. His humble posture isn't weakness—it's the very strength that allows true wisdom to flourish.

Let me encourage you, don't rush through this book, but rather savor and meditate upon it. You will be blessed as you slowly read these words and take in truths that help you to discern God's best for your life and for loving and serving others. Each devotional offers practical insights that bridge the gap between biblical truth and contemporary living. Whether you're facing major life decisions, seeking to grow in spiritual maturity, or simply wanting to walk more closely with God, Russell's gentle guidance will illuminate the path forward with wisdom that truly transforms.

Boyd Bailey
Wisdom Hunters And National Christian Foundation

Contents

Introduction

When I was a boy I spent my summers just off a country road at my Grandparent's home in the heart of Georgia. Oh the memories that were made digging in the red clay, muddy waters, and all under the oaks! During our summers, my brother and I would attend Vacation Bible School at the nearby country church. I mostly remember the snacks, building birdhouses, and playing outside. I think I put a new hole in my jeans everyday, and Grandma would patch them back up. During these formative summer days in the heat and humidity, I remember memorizing scriptures. This was the day with no fancy curriculum or catchy music to help you remember, but you just had to straight up memorize your verses.

Yeah, I was motivated with gold stars and mostly the candy, but I learned the Word. It was hidden in my heart from a young age. Like many of you who grew up with a similar background, I memorized and thereby meditated on Proverbs 3:5-6...

You can say it with me if you'd like...

Trust in the Lord with all your heart and lean not on your own understanding;

in all your ways acknowledge him, and he will make your paths straight.

Like a seed in the ground this promise has grown to bear much fruit in my life. Yet like my Grandma's garden, every good plant, vine, and tree must be pruned as it grows. You know about pruning, it doesn't feel good at the moment, but yields more fruit in time.

If we look closely at this promise from Proverbs, we see the work of both our heart and mind. But then it also talks about 'ways' and 'paths.' The implied idea is also physical, the doing, the walking out of God's will for our lives. Our trust and faith should encompass all parts of our everyday life just as the great commandment encourages, 'Love the Lord your God with all your heart, soul, mind, and strength.' It is in the seen and unseen dimensions of our living that we love the Lord and are loved by him. How well we love God and receive his love will influence how well we 'love our neighbor as ourself.' Or as Jesus also encourages us to "Love as I have loved you."

So back to our Proverbs passage, the word 'trust' is a soul response as we look to the Lord for answers as big as salvation for eternity, but also the grace just to walk through our day. The promise of Proverbs 3:5-6 challenges our faith that when we commit our heart, soul, mind to trusting and acknowledging the Lord, will He really direct our paths? The truth is that most of the time our daily circumstances and emotions leave us feeling the opposite.

There is a theme that I hear consistently from many men but really it's more of a heart cry, 'I'm stuck!' Last week a man I was meeting with said with hands raised in exhaustion and exasperation, 'God, what do you want me to do?' What's interesting about his story is that he's in pain and not from lack, but rather blessing. He is stewarding so much and needs wisdom from the Lord to direct his steps in his blessings. Yet, in the lack of direction, his heart cry reveals a painful anxiety that he doesn't know where he's going and therefore lacks the confidence for what to do today. So, as best as he can, he keeps his life in the center of the road and earnestly tries to manage his daily to do list.

I've met with hundreds of men, either in lack or abundance, all with the same painful heart cry asking, *where is all this going?* Can you relate? Do you have a clear call and direction from the Lord? Do you walk daily in confidence of who you are and what you are made to do? Do your circumstances create confusion in you? Or do you believe your choices have taken you off the path and you've lost hope?

Let me encourage you today....there is a way! Pray, meditate, and respond to this as a promise...

Trust in the Lord with all your heart and lean not on your own understanding;

in all your ways acknowledge him, and he will make your paths straight.

If you are stuck, plateaued, or in a fog of confusion with nowhere else to turn. Then it's time to trust. Take a step forward into the Lord's confidence. Find your way as you move towards his word, his work, and his ways. In pursuit of the Lord you will find him, then you will see him direct your paths.

It's a promise!

Wisdom on the Way was written during my season of transition. Many of these devotionals were written on days or during seasons when I lacked focus and direction. You could call them my darker days. I was searching more than any other time in my life. My friend and mentor Boyd Bailey calls it "Wisdom Hunting."

Woven throughout these devotionals are eight milestones from my life's journey that will hopefully serve as encouragement for you as you navigate overwhelming transitions, crises of confidence, and your milestone moments. These markers—from transformative love and marriage to entrepreneurship, fatherhood, major moves, career crossroads, and seasons of calling—represent the turning points that shaped my pursuit of wisdom. Each milestone reveals how God's faithfulness intersects with our willingness to take steps of faith, even when the path ahead seems uncertain.

Wisdom is found in the pursuit. You will find a consistent rhythm of writing, even a style that may seem a little repetitive. These daily entries are designed for reflection and meditation so that, in the end, you will find your heart leaning into the Lord a little further. As you encounter both the daily devotionals and the milestone moments scattered throughout, I pray that you find the wisdom and direction your heart desires—and perhaps recognize your own milestones along the way.

Victory On Bended Knee

There is no wisdom, no insight, no plan that can succeed against the Lord.—Proverbs 21:30

I've got spreadsheets, strategic plans, and a PowerPoint presentation that would impress anyone. I've thought through every angle, prepared for every objection, and strategized my way to what I believe is victory.

And then, in my hotel room the night before the big meeting, I feel it—that deep sense that **the most important thing I can do is pray.**

Not prepare more. Not rehearse again. Pray.

You'd think by my fifties I'd walk in this confidence naturally. But I don't. Even now, keeping in step with the Spirit feels like learning a new dance. I want to lean on my own understanding, trust my own genius, and control the outcome through sheer force of preparation.

But here's what I'm learning: **there is no wisdom, no insight, no plan that can succeed against the Lord.** Which means if God's not in it, my brilliant strategy is worthless. And if God is in it, my limited plans can't mess it up.

Look at the biblical pattern. Victory rarely came when Israel had the advantage. God specialized in impossible odds—outnumbered armies, untrained shepherds facing giants, walls falling from worship instead of warfare. Joshua's battle strategy at Jericho was circumcision and marching (Joshua 5-6). That's not tactics; that's trust.

The Lord's victory, achieved through our inability, defines our most powerful moments. Not when we muscled through. Not when our plans were flawless. When we were desperate, weak, out of options—and God showed up.

So why do I keep defaulting to self-reliance? Why do I power up my laptop before I bend a knee? Why do I muster strength instead of embracing weakness? Why do I strategize my way around fear instead of worshiping my way through it?

I'm preaching to myself here. When the board meeting looms and anxiety grips my chest, I need to worship first. When the presentation feels make-or-break, I need to pray first. When fear of circumstances threatens to paralyze me, I need to remember who God is—and let that fear of the Lord displace every other fear.

Do we need wisdom, insight, and planning? Absolutely. But first things first: **Where is the Lord at work?** That's the question that changes everything.

Because if He's not in it, all my preparation is just noise. And if He is in it, my weakness becomes the canvas for His strength. My inability becomes the stage for His glory. My bended knee becomes the position of true power.

The victories that matter most—in business, family, faith—don't come from perfect plans. They come from perfect surrender. From recognizing that no scheme of man can thwart what God wants to do, and no human wisdom can accomplish what only He can achieve.

Father, I confess I trust my plans more than Your presence. I lean on my understanding more than Your guidance. Teach me to bend my knee before I power up my presentations. Help me worship when fear grips me. Show me where You're at work so I can align my energy with Your purposes. Let victory come not from my strength but from surrendering to Yours. Keep me in step with Your Spirit today.

Let the Wise Learn and Discern

Let the wise listen and add to their learning, and let the discerning get guidance. —Proverbs 1:5

I watched wisdom in action with my friend Steve. At 50-something, navigating a significant life and career transition, Steve refused to let the fear of the unknown get the best of him. Rather than being paralyzed by uncertainty, he transformed the wait into his training ground. With the extra time he had in this transition, he took on a special interest and task of meeting with others to learn from their stories. He was living out what Proverbs 1:5 describes—listening intently and adding to his learning, seeking guidance with the heart of someone truly discerning.

Steve embodied this biblical principle beautifully. Every conversation became an opportunity to gather wisdom. He asked thoughtful questions about others' experiences, listened with genuine curiosity to their stories, and processed their insights as potential guidance for his journey. Rather than casual small talk, it's the disciplined pursuit of wisdom that prepares us for whatever God has planned.

How are you preparing today for what the Lord has for you tomorrow?

This question invites your focus on being present for today rather than preoccupation with the future. Too often, readiness means to us that we need to have complete clarity about our future. But Steve's example shows us something different: preparation is about cultivating the posture and practices that position us to receive God's guidance when we need it most. The wise, according to Proverbs, never stop learning.

They understand that even in seasons of waiting, there's work to be done. Steve's preparation looked like intentionally seeking out conversations with people who had walked similar paths. He listened to their victories and their regrets, their discoveries and their warnings. Each story became part of his preparation, adding layers of wisdom that would serve him well when decision time came.

The psalmist beautifully describes a wisdom posture as we step forward in faith, "Blessed are those whose strength is in you, who have set their hearts on pilgrimage" (Psalm 84:5). The pilgrimage mindset transforms waiting from passive anxiety into active preparation. Those who set their hearts on pilgrimage don't just endure uncertainty—they use it as a classroom for wisdom. Steve's approach revealed what proactive waiting is like. While others might worry about not having all the answers, he focused on becoming the kind of person who could recognize God's guidance when it came. He cultivated relationships with wise counselors, deepened his understanding of God's character through Scripture, and practiced the discipline of listening—both to God and to the people God had placed in his life.

The discerning, Proverbs tells us, actively seek guidance. They don't wait for wisdom to accidentally find them; they pursue it. They create learning opportunities, seek out mentors and advisors, and remain teachable regardless of their age or experience. Every season brings new crossroads requiring fresh wisdom. Who has God placed in your life to learn from? What questions could deepen your understanding of His ways? How will you actively listen and seek guidance as you prepare for tomorrow's opportunities?

Father, give me a teachable heart that transforms waiting into learning. Show me the wise counselors You've placed in my life and help me listen with genuine curiosity to their stories. Make me someone who actively pursues wisdom today so I'm ready to recognize Your guidance tomorrow.

The Cadence of Wisdom

Listen, my son, to your Father's instruction, and do not forsake your mother's teaching. They will be a garland to grace your head and a chain to adorn your neck. —Proverbs 1:8-9

L isten. Listen. Listen! Sharp, clear, distinctive words pierce through the noise of our busy lives. As you read Proverbs 1:1-7 aloud, notice the rhythm—a melody that flows from a father's heart. A cadence emerges, a pattern of action words ending in 'ING' that creates a drumbeat of engagement, demanding our participation in the pursuit of wisdom.

Written 3,000 years ago, these ancient words spark action today. Their wisdom transcends time, yet unlocking their treasure depends entirely on your posture of pursuit. Solomon warns that "the complacency of fools will destroy them" (1:32). To stagnate, to remain stuck, or to be crippled by fear leads only to spiritual slothfulness and the waywardness of the fool.

But there's another path—active waiting. We wait upon the Lord while pursuing Him with intentionality, understanding that wisdom comes to those who seek it with their whole hearts.

The Ten Action Words That Set the Cadence. Listen closely to these action words from Proverbs 1: *attaining, understanding, disciplining, acquiring, doing, giving, listening, learning, discerning,* and *beginning.* Each word pulses with movement, energy, and engagement. This cadence isn't passive wisdom—it's wisdom that requires your participation. These aren't merely intellectual concepts to be understood but active disciplines to be practiced. The rhythm builds momentum, creating a symphony of growth that transforms knowledge into lived experience.

Notice how these words interconnect: understanding flows from listening, disciplining leads to acquiring, and doing enables giving. The cadence creates a cycle of spiritual development where each action builds upon the previous one, propelling us forward in wisdom.

Where Are You Today?

Whatever your position, circumstance, or pain—no matter your past waywardness—remember this: "The fear of the Lord is the beginning of knowledge" (1:7). Today, His mercies are new. It's time to activate your faith and step into the rhythm of wisdom.

Turn from fear of circumstances to the fear of the Lord. There, you'll find His promises of wisdom, discipline, insight, prudence, righteousness, justice, fairness, learning, discernment, guidance, understanding, and knowledge. These aren't distant concepts but present realities available to those who pursue them.

The beauty of this cadence is that it meets you wherever you are. Whether you're beginning your journey of faith or have walked with God for decades, these action words call you deeper. The student finds new levels of understanding; the teacher discovers fresh insights to give.

The path of wisdom begins in pursuit of Him. Like a loving Father waiting to bless His child, He stands ready to place "a garland to grace your head and a chain to adorn your neck." These aren't mere ornaments but symbols of honor, beauty, and recognition that come from walking in wisdom.

Listen to the cadence. The call is clear: start now and take a step toward Him. Don't wait for perfect conditions or until you feel entirely ready. The wisdom you need is found in the pursuing, in the active engagement with His Word and His ways.

The action words aren't suggestions—they're invitations to a life of dynamic growth and transformation. Today, choose action over apathy, pursuit over passivity. Choose the cadence of wisdom over the silence of complacency.

Your Father is waiting. The garland of grace and chain of honor are ready. The rhythm of wisdom calls you forward into a life of purpose, growth, and divine favor.

What action word will define your next step?

Father, I hear Your call to pursue wisdom with my whole heart. Help me move beyond complacency into the active cadence of growth You've designed for me. Let me begin today with fresh faith, attaining the wisdom that comes from fearing You above all else. Guide my steps as I pursue You with intentionality and purpose.

Waywardness

For the waywardness of the simple will kill them, and the complacency of fools will destroy them, but whoever listens to me will live in safety and be at ease without fear of harm. —Proverbs 1:32-33

I 've been lost. Really lost. Not the lost where you take a wrong turn and need to check GPS—the kind where you wake up one morning and don't recognize the man in the mirror. The kind where fear has such a grip on your throat that you can't speak the truth to anyone, including yourself.

Whether I was simple, simple-minded, or simply a fool, I don't know. What I do know is this: I was wandering in circles, pretending I had a destination. My fear had gotten the better of my judgment, leaving me paralyzed at every crossroads. I was scared—terrified, actually—and desperately needed help to move from my fears to the refuge of safety promised by the Lord.

Looking back, waywardness nearly killed me. Not physically, but spiritually. I was dying a slow death of self-deception, building on sand while insisting the foundation was solid.

Have you lost your way? I don't mean occasionally confused—I mean genuinely lost. On a path you know is wrong but can't find the courage to turn around? Or worse, so comfortable with ignorance you've stopped asking hard questions altogether?

Let's be honest. Moving when you've been stuck takes everything. Looking at actual reality—not the story you've been telling yourself—requires brutal honesty. When you've squatted in the safe zone too long, you're not resting. You're dying.

That's where I was. In fog so thick I couldn't see my hand. Unless something changed, this fog would destroy everything.

The way out starts with **listening**. Not figuring it out. Not having your act together. Just listening.

I was the stubborn child insisting on my own way, straight into danger. What softened my heart? Realizing I was listening to all the wrong voices, including my own.

Write down your sources of counsel. Who influences your decisions? Some of my friends had joined me on the path of waywardness—not maliciously, they were just lost too. Waywardness loves an echo chamber.

I found three reliable sources: **Scripture**—living promises to stake your life on. **The Holy Spirit**—the voice that comforts, convicts, and empowers—the **Wise**—spiritual mentors, fathers, mothers, trusted friends who love you enough to tell the truth and help you move.

Here's the question: **Do you have death on you?** That spiritual death shows in your eyes, draining life from everything that matters.

If so, turn it over today. Confess your waywardness. Admit you're lost. The path of life is waiting—illuminated by Scripture, Spirit, and wise counsel.

But you must take the first step. Start listening. Start moving.

The promise? When you really listen, fear loses its grip. The fog clears. I know because I've walked out of it—one step at a time, listening to voices that knew the way.

Father, forgive my waywardness. Thank you, that it's not too late. Help me really listen today. Move me from death to life, fear to faith. Give me humility to receive counsel and courage to act. Let it start now.

Life Saving Wisdom

*Wisdom will save you from the ways of wicked men,
from men whose words are perverse.* —*Proverbs 2:12*

The promise is both stark and hopeful: wisdom will save you. But save you from what? Solomon provides a sobering list—wicked men, men of perversity, those who leave the straight path, who walk in dark ways, who delight in doing wrong. The catalog continues: perverseness of evil, crooked and devious paths, adulteresses with seductive words, covenant breakers, and those who traffic with the spirit of death.

This isn't abstract theology—it's practical reality. Every day, we encounter people and situations that could lead us astray. Some are obviously dangerous, but others are subtle, even attractive. The colleague who suggests cutting corners for profit. The friend who mocks your convictions. Online content slowly erodes your moral boundaries. The relationship that promises fulfillment but requires compromising your values.

Without wisdom, we're vulnerable to every deceptive voice and dangerous path. But with wisdom, we gain the ability to discern between truth and lies, between life-giving and death-dealing choices. Wisdom becomes our salvation from destruction.

How do we approach wisdom that will save us? Proverbs 2 provides a clear pathway: *Accept, Turn, Call, Look, and Understand.* These aren't passive activities but active pursuits that require intentional engagement.

Accepting means receiving God's words and storing them within us. We must value wisdom enough to welcome it into our hearts and minds. *Turn* means inclining our hearts toward understanding and making wisdom a priority in our decision-making. *Call* means crying aloud for insight and lifting our voices for understanding—actively seeking wisdom through prayer and study.

Look means searching for wisdom as we would search for silver and seeking it as we would seek hidden treasure. This suggests persistent, diligent effort. *Understanding* means truly comprehending the fear of the Lord and finding the knowledge of God. It's not just information but transformation.

When we act with this attitude—when we make the daily pursuit of wisdom our priority—then something remarkable happens. The Lord gives victory. He becomes a shield, guarding and protecting us along the way. This is the way of salvation, found in the pursuit of the One who gives wisdom to all who ask, seek, and find.

The beautiful promise at the end of Proverbs 2 is this: "Thus you will walk in the ways of good men and keep to the paths of the righteous." Wisdom doesn't just save us from destructive paths—it guides us toward life-giving ones. It connects us with people of integrity and keeps us on the trails that lead to blessing.

This salvation isn't a one-time event but an ongoing protection. Every day brings new challenges, new temptations, and new opportunities to either follow wisdom or fall into folly. However, as we continue to pursue wisdom, we continue to experience its saving power.

The enemy seeks to destroy us through deception, compromise, and a gradual drift away from the truth. But wisdom exposes his schemes and provides escape routes from his traps. Wisdom reveals the true character of people and situations, helping us avoid relationships and decisions that would harm us.

Wisdom is found in the pursuit of it. It's not a destination but a journey; not a de*gree, but a discipline. Those who pursue wisdom daily discover its saving power repeatedly.*

Father, I need Your wisdom to save me from the many dangers that surround me. Help me actively pursue wisdom through accepting Your Word, turning my heart toward understanding, calling out for insight, searching diligently for truth, and understanding Your ways. Be my shield and protection as I walk in wisdom's paths. Let me be a man of wisdom today and every day.

Milestone 1: Love That Never Fades

---◆◇◆---

L ife has its mile markers when we think of it in trail language. They're milestones—stacks of rocks that represent significant turning points or markers to show our progress along the way. As I share the wisdom gleaned from eight milestones in my life, I invite you to consider your defining moments as well - those crossroads that have shaped who you are today as you read.

My first milestone began during a pivotal summer when I traveled from Georgia to Montana to stay at my aunt and uncle's camp, Trails End Ranch. I was fourteen years old—a young buck full of myself convinced I had the world by the tail. I carried a certain arrogance that was off-putting to many people, not unlike many young men of that age. I thought I knew everything and acted accordingly. But something extraordinary happened during that summer. I found myself surrounded and nurtured by love—the patient love of my aunt, the wise counsel of my uncle, and perhaps most importantly, the friendships I developed with other young people at camp. Until that point, I'm not sure I knew what true friendship was.

What wrecked me: despite everything that was off-putting about me, these people loved me anyway. They loved me despite who I was and how I treated them. They saw past my arrogance and accepted me with unconditional love, an experience I had never had before. I had undoubtedly heard about the love of God in sermons and read about it in my Bible, but there was something about experiencing it through this group of people that changed everything. Something took hold in my heart that summer. Something ignited within my fourteen-year-old soul that I couldn't ignore or suppress.

Even today, I would call it a sense of calling—a deep, unshakeable conviction that I wanted to love people in the way that I had been loved. It was a living demonstration of what Jesus meant when he said, "Love one another as I have loved you." That commandment wasn't just words on a page anymore; it was lived out before my eyes, and I felt it in a very real way. That experience marked the beginning of my high school years and fundamentally changed my reputation. The Russell that people had known coming out of junior high—that guy was gone. I truly wanted to become someone who loved people, regardless of who they were or how they treated me. I wanted to love in the way that I had been loved.

That summer became a marker for my life, a fire that has remained constant throughout all these years. Despite hard times, difficult seasons, and even moments of spiritual drought, one thing has remained true: I have felt a deep calling to love people as I have been loved. This pursuit has been a constant in my life, and I've never wavered from it; for that, I thank God.

My milestone taught me that love—true, unconditional love—never fades. It transforms us, calls us to something greater than ourselves, and becomes the foundation upon which we build our lives. It's a constant, a source of comfort and reassurance in a world that is ever-changing.

What's that milestone in your life, that defining moment you would say was so core to who you are that it remains as accurate today as it was during that pivotal season? What love changed you forever? I encourage you to take a moment to reflect on your journey, your milestones, and the love that has shaped you.

Wisdom Walk

Thus, you will walk in the ways of good men and keep to the paths of the righteous. —*Proverbs 2:20*

D ave took time to model listening. Really listening. Not the kind where you're waiting for your turn to talk, but the kind where he'd ask me to share my story and then actually lean in. He'd ask follow-up questions. Remember details weeks later. He showed me what it meant to honor someone's story by giving it your full attention.

Tom opened my world beyond the borders of my American experience. He invited me on my first mission trip to Eastern Europe, where I learned to honor cultures completely different from my own. He modeled humility in unfamiliar places, respect for people who lived differently, and the beautiful reality that God's kingdom is far bigger than my comfortable corner of Colorado Springs.

Paul pursued time with me for over a year, inviting me to learn about leadership and mentorship firsthand. Not through books or seminars, but through life. Coffee meetings. Hard conversations. Watching how he made decisions, handled conflict, and loved his family. He let me see behind the curtain of his life.

Who walks with you today that models wisdom?

When you see the words 'good men,' who comes to your mind? Take just a moment to consider a few good men or women who influenced you by their 'ways.'

Most leaders I meet have great people they admire from a position, office, or platform. Yet the question of 'good men' has to do with personal influence. What have you learned and put into practice from these mentors? Influence is just that: influence; it shapes your attitude, thought, and action.

Rarely are we truly shaped—dare I say transformed—by hearing a message or reading a great book. Instead, it's most often in the exchange of life together. **Every interaction is changing us.** These conversations are transforming us into the person we are becoming. We may develop our thinking and focus on messages or methods. No doubt, they are powerful tools. Yet, the most potent influence comes from a model of another person's life. *It's more caught than taught.*

Great leaders are first great followers, and authentic leadership creates devoted followers. As you influence others, consider: **Who are you following?** Whose example shapes your leadership?

While we all aspire to walk in Christ's ways, who in your life embodies those ways? Who models the character and wisdom you seek to develop? The leaders we follow today shape the leaders we become tomorrow.

The 'ways of good men' also have to do with **pace.** When we see the righteous, we have a little bit of chase in each of us, and the pursuit is good. Yet, the chase must have a pace.

So, if you're slow, pick up your feet—no more shuffling, let's move. If you're fast, beware of burnout and compromise in other areas, as you may become unbalanced. If you're unsure, ask your spouse or closest friend. They'll be happy to tell you. Find that cadence of a strong, steady stride on the path of the righteous.

There are times to stall, 'wait on the Lord,' or speed up 'run the race.' Yet, for many highly driven men and women, the issue of pace has to do with racing against something other than the Lord's direction. They are stalled or racing in fear, insecurity, or shame. **Let's shed these hindrances** and move to a cadence as we keep in 'step with the Spirit' (Galatians 5:25) today.

For if you have given your life to Christ and submitted your ways to the Lord, you are the 'righteous.' Go, walk in confidence today that the Spirit of the Lord leads you as you trust in Him. For those looking for direction, you may feel lost, not knowing the way to go. Trust in Christ today. Then, you will become the 'righteous' by His justifying grace and sanctified as you follow Him.

He will lead, guide, and give you direction. Now, look around your life, find the 'righteous,' learn their ways, 'keep to the path,' and walk in it.

Father, thank You for the men and women You've placed in my life. Help me walk with wisdom-keepers today. Show me who I'm becoming through the people I'm following. Give me the right pace—not too fast, not too slow—but in step with Your Spirit.

Prolonged Prosperity

My son, do not forget my teaching, but keep my commands in your heart, for they will prolong your life many years and bring you prosperity. —Proverbs 3:1-2

'My son,' anytime I hear those words, I sit a little straighter. When Dad called me, he had my attention, or if it's my full name, then was I'm likely in some trouble. Yet, 'my son' attunes my ear to hear, and I'm genuinely ready to listen. There is wisdom about to be imparted, and I want to hear it. Not everyone has the model of a good father or father figure who would speak these words. So, for the moment, quiet your heart and mind, and consider your Father in heaven who wants to share insights that give you a long life and prosperity. Regardless of age or ethnicity, everyone desires these benefits.

This week, I had the opportunity to attend a roundtable luncheon with local business leaders. We were working through a goals exercise that guides some holistic thinking on life and priorities. The categories include personal, family, business, ministry, and community. After these leaders wrote down some of their goals, I asked them to prioritize them and then consider who they would invite to walk with them to help them achieve them. Ironically, the majority of participants stated that their top priorities were spending more time with God and consistent Bible reading. These leaders face significant business and, in many cases, family challenges, yet they were drawn to the top priority of knowing God and His Word. What a wonderful discovery process for the team to recognize, share, and dedicate themselves to the Lord. So, to all those who resonate with a desire to lengthen and deepen your time with the Lord, I encourage you with the words of Solomon: it 'will prolong your life many years and bring you prosperity.'

Now, listen to the words of David, 'Blessed is the man...his delight is in the law of the Lord, and on his law he meditates day and night. He is like a tree planted by streams of water, which yields fruit in season and whose leaf does not wither. What he does prospers' (Psalm 1:1-3). When King Solomon writes the words 'my son,' he knows this language, for he has heard the same calling since childhood from his father, King David. These words are a clear promise of prolonged prosperity. Indeed, there are seasons that 'yield fruit' and others where the growth is deep within the roots of the soil.

Consider the season of your development and prosperity. Biblically speaking, *the definition of prosperity is what's happening in the person before it happens through the person.* You are blessed today if you remember his promises and yield your life to his commands. Embrace today a life of devotion to the Lord and his words. Then you will be like David as he declares, 'I run the path of your commands, for you have set me free' (Psalm 119:32). Take a little extra time to read and reflect on his promises, claim them as your own, and let the Father, Son, and Spirit bring you long, abundant life.

Father, when You call me "my son/daughter," help me sit straighter and truly listen to Your wisdom. Work Your prosperity deep in my heart. Give me devotion to Your Word that sets me free to run in the path of Your commands with joy.

Trust Trumps Understanding

————◆◇◆————

*Trust in the Lord with all your heart and lean not on
your own understanding.* —Proverbs 3:5

O h my, dear friend, these words hold life in the balance for the
believer. These words have been a treasured promise for so many
followers of God. The claim for its promise comes in difficult times when
the path may not be so clear. In doing so, you unlock a wealth of wisdom,
direction, and blessing under the Lord's direction. Yet, it may not feel
so in the moment. Circumstances are not always a good indicator for
understanding. For in them, *what I think often seems to be more governed
by what I feel.*

Let's take caution, for our emotions help move and drive us to action,
yet it may not always be in the best direction. When our feelings or
motives drive our decisions, we open ourselves to expectations that may
not be based on reality. Beware of fantasy or fiction that drives our
agenda. How many people do you know have been so hurt, broken, and
left wounded from unmet expectations? We all have misplaced trust in
people and have scars from the pain. Does that mean we vow never to
trust again? No, quite the opposite. We are invited to a new place and
trust in the Lord, who loves us and will lead us.

We are called to trust first before understanding. Yet, we should examine the biblical context more closely for a deeper understanding.
Proverbs 3:5 cautions us towards our 'own understanding'; yet the purpose of the Proverbs is 'for understanding words of insight' (1:2), 'for
understanding proverbs and parables' (1:6), 'apply your heart to un-

derstanding' (2:2), 'cry aloud for understanding' (2:3), to 'understand the fear of the Lord' (2:5), 'then you will understand what is right and just' (2:9), 'understanding will guard you' (2:11). God has given us great capacity in heart, mind, and spirit to understanding. We are cautioned, rather charged, not to 'lean not on your own understanding.' Yet, the very purpose of the proverbs invites us to understand.

The very essence of wisdom and, therefore, understanding comes in fear of the Lord above fear of people and circumstances. When your focus is on the Lord above, the details of the challenges you face will take a backseat, and you will have a clearer perspective on what is right, which will guard you. As a Spirit-filled believer, God has given you a great gift, 'we have the mind of Christ' (1 Corinthians 2:16). There is understanding for the asking, seeking, and trusting. *What cripples understanding is fear rather than faith and trust in our resources rather than in the Lord.*

We are called to a life of wisdom, which implies mandates, seeking, and crying out for understanding. Yet, in your pursuit, find rest for your souls in trusting the Lord. Let us not be like the man the Psalmist describes, 'who did not make God his stronghold but trusted in his great wealth' (Psalm 52:7). Let us pursue understanding yet yield to the trust of the Lord. Let us declare, 'I trust in God's unfailing love' (8), 'I will praise you,' 'I will hope,' and 'I will praise you' (9). God is good; he loves you, and his grace will sustain you abundantly. 'Trust in the Lord with all your heart' today.

Trust trumps understanding of God's purposes, which are greater than our own.

Father, I confess I want to understand before I trust. Help me anchor my trust in Your character instead of my clarity. Give me rest in knowing Your purposes are greater than my understanding, and Your love is more reliable than my limited perspective. I will trust you today!

Force For Good!

Do not withhold good from those to whom it is due,
when it is in your power to act. —*Proverbs 3:27*

I remember the weight of an empty bank account when bills were due. The shame of carefully calculating every grocery store purchase, putting items back at the register because the total was too high. The anxiety of watching the gas gauge drop while managing cash flow between projects that felt like they'd never pay.

Then someone saw our need and stepped in.

A grocery gift card was left anonymously in our mailbox. We got restaurant gift certificates for date nights when we hadn't been out in months. A mechanic friend, who learned about our vehicle's heating system, died in the middle of winter and just showed up to fix it. Another who saw how dangerously thin my truck tires were getting and bought a new set—not a loan, a gift—to keep me safe on the road.

I'm sobered even now, remembering those moments. Grateful. **Moved to tears** thinking about how vulnerable I felt during those days, yet how deeply loved. People saw our struggle and didn't look away. They didn't wait for us to ask—they just acted when it was in their power to act.

Those moments changed me. They didn't just meet a need—they showed me what generosity actually looks like. It's not about grand gestures or tax-deductible donations, but about seeing someone in need and doing something about it immediately.

Now I think differently about even the smallest ways to serve, love, and bless others. Our family carries a mantra: **"We are blessed to be a blessing."** We know what it is to be lacking. We remember what it felt like to wonder if we'd make it. We hope we can help others feel loved and supported, even in the smallest ways.

Paul writes that "such acts of generosity result in thanksgiving to God" (2 Corinthians 9:11). That's the beautiful multiplier effect—when you withhold good, everyone loses. When you give, everyone gains. The receiver is blessed. You're blessed. And God gets the glory.

So here's my challenge: Whatever you can give, give it without hesitation. When it's in your power to act, act. Don't wait for the perfect moment or the perfect amount. Just do it.

But here's the harder question: **What's holding you back?** Stubbornness? Laziness? Contempt for people you think should figure it out themselves? Pride that says your resources are yours alone?

Repent of any selfishness or scarcity mindset. Break free from the lie that giving diminishes you. Because here's the truth: I've lived on both sides, and you may find that you receive a blessing in ways you never expected.

Father, forgive my hesitation to give when I have the power to act. Break any scarcity mindset in me. Open my eyes to the needs around me today. Make me a force for good—blessing others the way I've been blessed. Let my generosity result in thanksgiving to You.

Cost of Understanding

————◆◆◆————

Wisdom is supreme; therefore, get wisdom. Though it costs you everything, be understanding. —Proverbs 4:7

'Ready, fire, aim' leaders are prone to adapt and improvise. It's a noble characteristic to take action even if misguided or misdirected. Yet, those experienced leaders with this style of operation don't have to look too far back to see the negative effects of acting without understanding. There is also equal danger in taking no action. Bad experiences and costly mistakes are great trainers, yet without understanding, they can cripple us towards taking any action. Then, we are stuck with indecision. We are wounded from past efforts, and then the faith and courage to move forward seems too great. What used to be easy now requires so much more effort to take the initiative to decide and act. Some may be bound by 'analysis paralysis.' Whatever has caused you to stumble, even lose your way, God offers wisdom and understanding for the asking.

What is the cost of understanding? Can you measure cost in terms of your time, money, or other resources? *A wise mentor shared with me that experiences do not make you wise; it's the evaluation of experiences that makes you wise.* Taking the time to evaluate your experience will cost you. Asking tough questions and inviting others into the process may risk embarrassment or lead to encouragement from the leader and the team being evaluated. The same principle applies within a family; we all have experiences and daily lessons that can be learned. Yet, they can be passed over if not discussed together. *Wisdom and understanding come from the discovery of evaluated experience.*

Take the necessary time to invite feedback about your experience. Invite team members or family to discuss specific situations. Often, experiences that feel like complete failures can be turned into a wealth of wisdom and understanding. Yet, these treasures lay in the darkness waiting to be discovered. Only shame, discouragement, and distrust stand in the way of their riches. Will you have the courage to press into the perceived darkness of a bad experience with a trusted few? No doubt it will cost you; the most significant cost may be your pride. For in the pursuit of wisdom and understanding, the most excellent posture we can adopt is one of humility and a recognition of our need for grace. Wisdom and understanding await you. 'Esteem her, and she will exalt you; embrace her, and she will honor you' (4:8).

Consider the cost of unevaluated experiences. Consider the cost of repeated mistakes, for these costs far outweigh the investment of time and resources required. The benefits of understanding will 'exalt' and 'honor' you. Your character will develop. Trust will mature in a relationship. Consider today who can walk with you in pursuit of understanding and wisdom. 'Though it cost you all you have'; what will be the cost if you don't?

Wisdom and understanding come from the discovery of evaluated experience.

Father, give me courage to evaluate my experiences honestly instead of just surviving them and moving on. Humble my pride enough to invite trusted people into my failures. Help me pay the cost of understanding today and avoid repeating the same mistakes tomorrow.

Guard Your Heart

Above all else, guard your heart, for it is the wellspring of life. —Proverbs 4:23

E arlier this week, while driving away from a high-intensity meeting with some local leaders, I felt exhausted. I served from my passion, strength, and skill set. Several attendees from the meeting offered their thanks. They shared some personal insights and action steps. Although I was encouraged and grateful for the opportunity to serve, I was exhausted. Then, before I was 10 minutes down the road, my mind flooded with a list of to-dos awaiting my attention. My instincts were screaming, I hit the redline, and I knew I was crashing. At that moment, a question arose in my mind: *what do I do to refresh myself?* First, nothing came to mind because I had exhausted all my creative energy. I prayed and asked the Lord to refresh me. Then, a thought came: take a nap, go for a swim, or laugh with your kids. It's 2 pm on a Thursday; kids are busy, so a nap sounds good, but I wait until Saturday. So, I go for a swim.

So I did... After my swim, I experienced such clarity, focus, and energy that I finished out my day truly productive. During my laps in the pool, I realized my week had been filled with about 12 things that had utterly exhausted me, so my 'power lunch' was the tipping point of my crash. I thank God for the wisdom and realization that I needed to 'guard my heart.' There are times when I have felt 'exposed' or too vulnerable from exhaustion or managing a crisis that opens the door to some destructive thinking and attitudes. In those times, I know my 'wellspring' has run dry.

Where are you today, overflowing with life, or has your wellspring run dry? Consider the words and counsel of 'above all else.' For it speaks of priority and primary focus. If you compromise, the door of your heart opens just a little to a host of voices, influences, and, dare I say, 'lies' that would take the very life from you. These words and this charge to you carry a significant weight, for you matter! You are loved, made righteous, and called into the family of God as a son or daughter. You have a purpose (Psalm 139) and a destiny that God has designed for you (Ephesians 2:10).

God's building a Kingdom that we all will be celebrating together one day, on 'that day.' We live life today in light of eternity. When our heart is not guarded, we forget all these promises. Life becomes one of mediocrity and maybe even survival. For there is a battle, Paul writes to believers with these words. *'Be on your guard;* stand firm in the faith; be men of courage; be strong' (1 Corinthians 16:13). Let us be wise to what wars against us, wears us down, and leaves us exposed. Claim the promises of God, stir up faith and the gifts of the Spirit, and surround yourself with other believers who will stand with you, for we were never meant to do this alone (Hebrews 10:24-25). Ask the Lord for wisdom, insight, and understanding so you may answer, how do I guard my heart? Let us pray today like David,

Father, teach me to recognize when I've hit the redline before I crash completely. Show me what refreshes my soul and give me permission to stop and renew myself in you — guard my heart. Don't let exhaustion drain my wellspring; keep me full of Your life today.

The Path We Make for Others

"Give careful thought to the paths for your feet and be steadfast in all your ways." —Proverbs 4:26

P aths have become a recurring biblical theme in my reflections these past months, and this morning, I understand why. The imagery is inescapable—we're all walking somewhere, and more importantly, we're all creating paths for others to follow.

The writer of Hebrews builds on Solomon's wisdom. *Therefore, strengthen your feeble arms and weak knees. Make level paths for your feet, so that the lame may not be disabled, but rather healed.* - Hebrews 12:12-13. Our paths don't just affect us. They either help or harm those following behind us.

The metaphor is vivid and convicting. Picture someone walking through rough terrain with "feeble arms and weak knees"—perhaps injured, exhausted, or struggling to keep up. Now imagine you're walking ahead of them, and the path you choose will determine whether they make it safely or stumble and fall. If you pick your way carefully, clearing obstacles and choosing stable footing, you create a "level path" that enables their healing and progress. But if you're careless, distracted, or reckless, you leave behind a treacherous trail that could disable them permanently.

This reality has been weighing heavily on my heart lately: My commitments will either cripple or enable others. The stakes are incredibly high. Every decision I make, every priority I set, and every standard I maintain or compromise on creates a path that others will follow. My children watch how I handle stress and learn their own coping mechanisms. My colleagues observe how I conduct business and form their own ethical framework. My friends see how I navigate marriage and gain insights into their own relationships.

The responsibility feels overwhelming at times. How do I ensure I'm creating paths that lead to healing rather than harm? How do I strengthen my own "feeble arms and weak knees" so I can clear the way for others?

First, I must seek wisdom to navigate potential pitfalls while listening clearly to God's leading. Wisdom isn't just for my benefit—it's for everyone walking in my footsteps. When I make poor choices, the consequences ripple outward, creating obstacles for those who look to me as an example.

Second, I need to honestly assess whether God has granted me the grace, favor, and provision necessary for the path I'm on. Sometimes, we attempt to blaze trails we're not equipped to handle, creating dangerous routes for those following behind. Humility requires acknowledging our limitations and staying within the boundaries of God's calling and provision.

Third, I must pray for clarity to see, hear, and understand God's direction clearly. The Hebrew writer uses active verbs—"make" and "take"—suggesting that we have a responsibility to create our own path. God provides the direction, but we must actively choose to follow it and intentionally prepare the way for others.

Who is following your path today? What kind of trail are you leaving behind? Are you strengthening your own spiritual condition so you can clear the way for others' healing, or are you creating obstacles that might disable those already struggling?

Father, strengthen my feeble arms and weak knees so I can make level paths for those following behind me. Give me wisdom to navigate safely and clarity to hear Your leading. Help me be a path-maker who leads others well today.

Milestone 2: The Love of My Life

When I met Cari Lynn Regehr. We knew each other from our high school youth group, but our friendship truly began during a mission trip in the Appalachian Mountains of eastern Kentucky. Working together on that ministry team, we were assigned to the same construction work team, and suddenly, we had the opportunity to discover who each other was beyond the familiar faces in the youth group. Thus, a friendship started.

Later, during our college years, we had the chance to meet again through my now brother-in-law, Scott Northway. After that Bible study and our first official date, sparks started flying. I'll be honest—we had a rocky start, primarily because Cari wasn't entirely sure about me. I was a lot to handle even then, carrying the same intensity that had marked my younger years.

As those sparks flew, something ignited that would prove life-changing. Cari became the love of my life, and she has been for over thirty years of marriage now. She's my best friend, my sweetheart, my wife, my partner. When we later explore Proverbs 31 and the concept of wisdom, she models 'lady wisdom' in the flesh. This transformative power of love, rooted in faith, has sustained us through the years.

One of the routines that has sustained our marriage over the years is our morning coffee dates. Each day begins with me bringing her coffee or tea, and we share early morning conversations before our day unfolds. This simple rhythm nurtures our hearts, gives us space to listen and care for one another, and helps us set our priorities together. It's become a sacred time that anchors everything else.

Cari is the woman I trust most in this world. I rely on her intuition, her discernment, and the insight God gives her because she is a woman who prays for me. What an incredible privilege that is. I know all too well that not everyone has this kind of marriage, and I'm deeply grateful.

Over the years, our shared pursuit of the Lord, His word, and wisdom has translated into a deep heart for God and for one another that truly sustains our marriage. There are countless things I love about Cari and our life together—adventure, fun, laughter, living a life of faith, overcoming challenges, facing difficult days, and still extending grace to one another.

But the common denominator is our life of prayer, our pursuit of the Lord, and our commitment to seeking His word together. Now, even in this season of life, we have the joy of being ministry partners, mentoring, and caring for other people together. Our shared pursuits bring us joy and keep our bond strong.

At the core of our love for one another is the pursuit of wisdom. Cari is the love of my life, and my encouragement to those desiring a whole and healthy marriage is this: it's not about perfection, but about being present with one another and pursuing wisdom together. Being present in a relationship is a powerful way to show love and understanding.

Come Clean! Lest You Give Your Best!

Lest you give your best strength to others and your years to one who is cruel. —Proverbs 5:9

There is great strength waiting in the reserves of men and women, yet it's veiled in weakness. Weakness caused by compromise. Now, we sit in the shadows and still feel shame from our past. For our very best has been given to another not worthy of it. The lure of lust and pride at the moment has beaten some of the best of men. Even the strongest and most resolute can be overcome by fatigue and weakness. Be aware in these moments that we are at risk of our desires. Our desires can compromise our convictions and character. When we do, there is a shroud of shame and the guilt of specific thoughts or actions that led us to give our best strength to others. In a compromised life, there can be nothing more cruel than an unclean conscience.

Who has given their best to the lure of the unrighteous? Who has a compromised conscience? Let scripture answer the question, 'for all who sinned and fall short of the glory of God' (Romans 3:23). For its lure and cause is common for all men. Solomon writes a sobering and 'cruel' account in chapters 5-7 of a path that leads only to 'death' (7:27). It's a progression from desire to death. (James 1:14-15). For desire has a definition rooted in these 3: 'the lust of the flesh, the lust of the eyes, and the pride of life—comes not from the Father but from the world.' (1 John 2:16). *Take a moment, quiet your soul, silence the cruelty, and let the fog clear of ambiguity. Let the Spirit of God minister to you with grace, forgiveness, and love, for you are not meant to carry any longer the weight of shame and guilt. Come clean with your desire for lust and pride. Come out from under its yoke and burden of cruelty, for you are a slave to its power no longer. Say with me out loud, pray, and claim this promise for your own today,* 'If we confess our sins, He is faithful and just and will forgive us our sins and purify us from all unrighteousness' (1 John 1:9).

By your claim and confession, you are forgiven! Now, go and sin no more!

You are righteous in God's sight. You shed the cloak of weakness found in shame. You take on the garment of grace. Strengthen yourselves in the confidence of faith, for you are clean! For you are pure! For you are righteous! *Give your best strength in love and humility, and guard yourselves to lust and pride.* God's abundant grace will be poured out on you today for the asking. Your life is no longer marked by compromise and cruelty. Instead, you have been called to conviction and confidence.

Live each day empowered by God's grace rather than weakened by past failures. When you encounter others trapped in shame's harsh grip, become a channel of God's liberating grace. Come alongside fellow believers who are struggling—strengthen and encourage them so they too can discover the power that comes from walking in grace rather than guilt. Your days and years should be defined not by past mistakes, but by the strength that flows from God's unending grace.

Forgiveness opens the heavens of grace to clean your consciousness and renew your strength.

Father, I confess the desires of lust and pride that have compromised my strength and left me sitting in shame's shadows. Thank You that Your forgiveness is complete—purifying me from all unrighteousness and clothing me in grace instead of guilt. Renew my strength today so I can give my best to what's worthy, living empowered by Your grace rather than crippled by my past.

Corrective Discipline

How I hated discipline! How my heart spurned correction! —Proverbs 5:12

Those who hate discipline and correction often end up hating themselves. It's a strong statement, but significant when we understand that discipline and correction save us from destruction.

Watch a six-year-old at bedtime when it's time to brush their teeth. The threshold of discipline seems unreasonable—why does this matter so much? Because if you don't, cavities are coming. Simple. Painful. Expensive. The child hates the discipline now, but will hate the dentist's drill more later.

I was that thirteen-year-old who couldn't turn homework in on time. It seemed like such a small thing—what's one late assignment? What's another zero in the gradebook? I hated the correction from teachers, the discipline of deadlines, and the accountability of checking my backpack every night. That rebellion set a trend for the rest of my high school days, tanked my GPA, and limited my post-graduation options. I paid the price for years because I spurned correction when it could have saved me.

The sixteen-year-old gets their license and suddenly feels that the rules on the road are restrictive. Speed limits, stop signs, turn signals—all unnecessary discipline until the day it costs you. Your insurance rate. Your clean driving record. Maybe worse.

Then there's the twenty-six-year-old fresh out of college, who finally landed a job making real money, and gets carried away with credit cards.

The discipline of budgeting feels boring compared to buying what you want when you want it until debt compounds. You will be paying hundreds in interest every month. Until you can't buy a home, can't take a vacation, can't give to someone in need because you're drowning in payments for purchases you barely remember making.

These aren't hypothetical examples. They're the predictable results of hating discipline and spurning correction. To ignore counsel, reject authority, and dismiss accountability reveals a rebellion that always comes at a cost.

Here's what I've learned the hard way: coming under authority—submitting to discipline and correction—"yields a harvest of righteousness and peace for those who have been trained by it" (Hebrews 12:11). No discipline is pleasant at the time. It feels restrictive, annoying, and unnecessary. But it's the training ground for a good life.

The six-year-old who learns to brush their teeth. The thirteen-year-old who turns homework in on time. The sixteen-year-old who follows traffic laws. The twenty-six-year-old who lives within their means. They're all learning the same lesson at different levels: **discipline now prevents destruction later.** Consider the corrective discipline you need to heed today that will bring a good return in your future.

Father, forgive my rebellion against discipline. Help me see correction as protection, not punishment. Give me humility to receive counsel and wisdom to submit to authority. Train me through discipline so I can harvest righteousness and peace instead of regret.

Consider the Ant

Go to the ant, you sluggard; consider its ways and be wise! —*Proverbs 6:6*

I hate ants! At least I did when I was a kid. Growing up in Georgia, they'd come up from the red clay in full force to devour your lunch, protect their hill, or take you out at the ankles. As a young boy, after stepping in a few ant hills and feeling the effects of my poor judgment, I would retaliate in force. I would destroy their little home with sticks and rocks and, finally, drown the little community with a water hose. 'That'll show 'em,' I think. Then, a week or so later, the same community had moved its headquarters to the backside of the pine tree. Then, if left alone, the next hill would be bigger than the first. It seemed like a losing battle for a young boy on a mission, never to be bitten again.

Consider the ant! When I let my boyhood battle cry subside and disregard the memories of watermelon being hauled off by the slice, OK, I'll consider the ant! I will learn from my enemy! Here are a couple of observations from the ways of an ant.

- No commander- Leadership by Mission. Develop the colony by building infrastructure, preparing for food and shelter in season, and always marching in a single line. Overcome and rebuild when disaster strikes. They are clear and committed.

- No ruler- Diligent Workers. They work like slaves, but they have no masters. They have a job and get it done. They work together and rarely alone.

- No overseer- Self and Team Management. Work together for a common goal, share the load when it gets too heavy, care for the injured, and have an internal drive to complete what they start. They are organized and efficient.

Solomon compares the nobility of the ant to the sluggard. The lazy man, or sluggard, will reap what he sows in the forms of 'poverty' and 'scarcity' (11). Being from the south, knocking over ant hills, I also saw the slow, slimy trails of a slug on a sidewalk. What a pitiful creature. It's lazy and slow, and whenever anything happens, it crawls into its shell for protection. It's immobilized by fear and self-protection. The slug rarely travels in the community. It's slim and odor-repelling, keeping anyone away. No one wants to be a sluggard.

Now, consider the ant; there is another extreme. For they are workaholics, their vices run deeper than just good work ethic. They are running, driven by another master. Let me encourage you: there is freedom from that fear of failure. Your sense of worth and identity comes from who you are as a child of God. What you do for work is an expression of who you are and not your identity. You are worth more than your work! Your value comes from more than what you can produce. Consider the balance of the ant who works in season, preparing in a time of harvest and winter rest. Consider the ways of the ant. *Learn from their consistency of work, commitment to mission, and community to strengthen.* Confess your laziness or procrastination. Get organized and get moving! Despite my troubled boyhood, my enemy has become my teacher.

Consider the ways of the ant and be wise.

Father, save me from both the sluggard's laziness and the workaholic's fear-driven frenzy. Remind me my worth comes from being Your child, not from what I produce. Give me the ant's diligent work ethic balanced with rest, community, and clear mission.

Detestable Dissension

*There are six things the Lord hates, seven that are
detestable to him... a person who stirs up conflict in the
community.—Proverbs 6:16-19*

I 've been part of only two churches my entire adult life since I was 15
years old. Two churches in nearly four decades. And I can't count
how many times I could have had an easy excuse to leave—legitimate
reasons to pack up and find somewhere "better."
It's so easy to take offense that leads to division. A disagreement
over ministry direction. A comment that felt personal. A leadership
decision you disagreed with—a conflict with another member. In today's church culture, we've made it normal to leave at the first sign of
discomfort, spreading our complaints as we go.

But here's what stops me cold: **God hates dissension.** Not dislikes.
Not disapproving of. Hates. He lists seven detestable things, and the
last one, which He emphasizes, is "a person who stirs up conflict in the
community."

A person who sows dissension breeds destruction and fosters conflict.
Yikes! No one wants that on their resume. Yet Christians can be the most
divisive group of people. Social media has become a platform where believers publicly criticize each other, stirring up skepticism and suspicion.
A simple negative comment becomes a destructive tool, spreading hate
like cancer through communities, churches, families, and workplaces.

Jesus' biggest prayer before the cross was that we would be one,
brought to complete unity. Today, I see people church-hopping at the

drop of a hat, spreading complaints, sowing seeds of discontent. I see teenagers losing their spiritual footing because their families can't stay in one church long enough to put down roots.

One of the most painful experiences of my life was being falsely accused. What started as whispers grew into slander that required mediation with our pastor. Being slandered felt like it took years off my life. My work suffered. Trust shattered.

Paul warns us in Ephesians 4:30-31: **"Do not grieve the Holy Spirit of God... Get rid of all bitterness, rage, and anger, brawling and slander."** When we slander others—speaking false or damaging words about fellow believers—we're not just hurting them. We're grieving the Holy Spirit who lives in us.

Here's the painful irony: the very forgiveness we beg from the Lord—"forgive us our debts"—we withhold from others. How can we pray the Lord's Prayer asking God to forgive us "as we forgive those who trespass against us" while harboring bitterness and stirring up conflict?

The Lord loves it when we love one another, when we come together in unity. When we let go of offenses. Proverbs 17:9 tells us that whoever covers an offense seeks love, but repeating a matter separates friends.

The challenge is simple but not easy: Seek understanding and reconciliation. Romans 12:18 says, "If it is possible, as far as it depends on you, live at peace with everyone." You can't control their response, but you can control yours—your words, your willingness to reconcile, your refusal to sow dissension or slander.

Father, forgive me for stirring up conflict and grieving Your Spirit through slander. Help me let go of offenses and seek reconciliation where I've been wronged. Let me be a peacemaker, not a dissension-sower.

A Free Commodity

*When you walk, they will guide you; when you sleep
they will watch over you; when you awake they will
speak to you. — Proverbs 6:22*

On my first visit to China, I met a remarkable missionary who
had spent decades smuggling Bibles and resources to the underground church. During our lunch near Hong Kong harbor, she shared miraculous stories of believers throughout Asia—tales that stirred my faith and expanded my vision of God's work around the world. Her ministry had influenced literally millions of new believers and fueled the expansion of the church in the most restrictive circumstances.

During one of her stories, she made a statement that gripped me: "Wisdom is a free commodity; only a fool wouldn't buy it." Her metaphor was particularly striking given our location in Hong Kong's financial district, surrounded by the world's most expensive real estate and exclusive trading floors. Here was a woman who understood actual value—wisdom is available to anyone for a price we can all afford. It's waiting for us to seek it out, pursue it passionately, and discover its immeasurable worth. God has promised to give wisdom generously to all who ask without finding fault.

Solomon's promise reveals that when we receive wisdom, it doesn't remain dormant—it begins active work in our lives. Wisdom operates around the clock, engaging with us in the natural rhythms of each day. Consider how wisdom wants to work in your life today across three essential phases: awakening, walking, and sleeping.

When You Awake

What were the first thoughts that crossed your mind this morning? Your answer reveals what occupies your heart—praise, prayers, promises, plans, pain, or panic. Each new day carries its own weight of anticipation and temptation to worry over events and details beyond our control. But when we've filled our minds with God's wisdom, those first conscious moments become opportunities for His voice to speak direction, comfort, or clarity into our day. Instead of awakening to anxiety, we can awaken to wisdom's counsel.

When You Walk

Consider your responsibilities, commitments, and the various roles you'll play today. You wear many hats—parent, spouse, employee, leader, friend. Each role brings decisions, challenges, and opportunities to demonstrate wisdom or folly. As you navigate meetings, conversations, and unexpected situations, wisdom promises to guide your steps. This isn't passive guidance but active direction—wisdom helps you choose the right words in difficult conversations, make sound decisions under pressure, and respond with grace when others disappoint you.

When You Sleep

Even in rest, wisdom continues its work. While you sleep, God's truth watches over you, protecting your heart and mind from the enemy's lies. The worries that seemed overwhelming at bedtime lose their power when placed under wisdom's protective watch. Peaceful sleep often comes not from solved problems but from surrendered concerns—trusting that divine wisdom is working even when we're not conscious.

Solomon concludes this section with a beautiful metaphor: "These commands are a lamp; this teaching is a light." Wisdom illuminates our path in darkness, reveals hidden dangers, and shows us the way forward when circumstances seem confusing.

The missionary in Hong Kong understood what many miss—wisdom isn't merely information to be collected but transformation to be experienced. It's a living guide that speaks, directs, and protects throughout every season of life. The question isn't whether wisdom is available but whether we're willing to invest in this priceless commodity that costs nothing but yields everything.

Father, thank You for making wisdom freely available to all who seek it. Help me awaken each day ready to hear Your voice, walk each step guided by Your truth, and sleep each night under Your protective care. Make me a wise investor in the only commodity that genuinely matters.

Keep and Store

My son, keep my commands and store them within you. —*Proverbs 7:1*

H ow many sons and daughters are reading this post today? If you are a son or daughter, say, 'I am a son- I am daughter' Then, my brother and sister, these words are for us today. When I see and hear these words, I sit a little straighter. A friend of mine shared with me, 'Listen well to the words of advice from older men, for it costs them." When you read Proverbs 7 and read through the story of Solomon's life, what was the cost of the wayward woman? For the richest king in history, it cost him dearly. Tender and strong words of advice come at a cost. Listen carefully to its counsel. The call, 'my son,' speaks words of identity and life. 'My son' speaks a claim over you by your father. No matter the depth of blessings or cursings spoken over you by your Dad or father figures, your Heavenly Father wants to speak words of life to you now. 'My son,' receive the wisdom from the father today. Let Him speak beyond these written words to the heart and soul, the words you most need to hear today.

'Keep' and 'Store,' even the most reflective men and women at some point need to take action. There is a time to wait and be patient for instruction and direction. For if we move too quickly, it's likely to be off course. Some of us feel as if we've been off course most of our lives. Wherever you are today on the journey, listen to the instructions and action steps from the father.

Why? 'Keep my commands, and you will live' (7:2). If you continue reading Proverbs 7, you will quickly note that your life may depend on it. The counsel of the word protects you when you are tempted to stray. What will keep you on the path of life today? *The commands of the Lord are the promises of God in which He reveals His power in your life when you believe.*

You are smart, creative, even strategic. It's the way your mind works. Take counsel from the father today. Then consider and act on the charge to 'keep' and 'store.' Create an action plan to take hold of the promises of God. Throughout the day, you visually can see its counsel that it would penetrate your heart, guard your mind, and be the voice of encouragement from your mouth. Your mind and heart can be a warehouse of promises just waiting to be called upon by the Holy Spirit when you need it most. Disregard and silence the voice in your head that says, 'I can't memorize the Bible.' You can start today with one verse in your pocket or on your phone.

Let it be your theme for the week. Then, choose another the following week. Then, by year-end, you can say, 'Father, I have kept and stored your promises.' When you do, you will know the wisdom in your heart, for you will be a wise son. Let us start today with 'keep' and 'store.' For your life may depend on it.

'I run in the path of your commands, for you have set my heart free' (Psalm 119:32).

Commands of God are promises waiting to reveal freedom and power in your life.

Father, I receive Your words as a beloved son/daughter today—speak life and wisdom directly to my heart. Help me keep and store Your promises like a warehouse ready for the Holy Spirit to access when I need them most. Set my heart free today as I run in the path of Your commands.

Looks that Kill

At the window of my house, I looked out through the lattice. —Proverbs 7:6

Years ago, early one morning, my son crawled in my lap. Still sleepy from his slumber and wrapped in his blanket, he sat quietly for a moment. As I read, he looked at the pages, then asked,' Daddy, why is that word *WARNING* randomly written in red in your bible?' 'Good question, son, let me read a little to you from Proverbs 7.' My son was 8. I pray he will heed its warning as as a man.

Notice the language of the proverbs - 'window' and 'lattice.' See where this story begins for the young man on his journey that will only end in destruction. In his home and hiding behind the lattice. He was already hiding before he came out of his house. What did the man do? He 'looked.' *The progression of promiscuity begins at the heart, entertained by the mind, and the first act with the eyes.* The eyes are the window to the soul. Paul prays, 'I pray that the eyes of your heart may be enlightened' (Ephesians 1:18). We truly want what brings light and, therefore, life, for we know all too well when our heart is in darkness, and we begin looking 'through the lattice' to satisfy the lust of our heart. It's been taught that lust is simply an unmet emotional need. All of our hearts long to be loved, but let us not settle for second-hand love.

How many sons, young and old, are sitting in the shadows of their homes feeling unloved? For those of us strong in the faith, let us bless these men and model the Father's grace, forgiveness, and love for them. How many daughters are like the ones in Proverbs 7, seeking to find love in the only way she knows? Let us look into the eyes of our daughters and remind them of the beauty within and speak life, light, and love over their darkened souls.

Let us all heed the counsel of the scriptures, 'Keep my commands and you will live' (2). The road that this young man followed is marked, 'her house is the highway to the grave, leading down to the chambers of death' (27). Be careful not to trust your counsel in this matter alone. The old idiom is true: *the road to hell is paved with good intentions.* Let us first consider what our eyes see. What are you looking at for too long? What has captured your attention beyond what is righteous?

Beware of the look that kills! For we all have idols! Let us remove the idols from our hearts and homes, then turn our worship to the one true God. Let us share our confession with a trusted few, receive their supportive counsel, and together celebrate worship to God. Turn your eyes away from whatever screen or 'lattice' that keeps you hidden in shame. Turn your heart back to the lover of our souls. For today, He wants to speak life, light, and love to you once again.

Father, enlighten the eyes of my heart so I see Your goodness instead of looking through the lattice for cheap substitutes of love. Remove the idols from my heart and home, surround me with faithful people who will walk with me in purity, and replace every lure of lust with the endless love of Christ. Turn my eyes away from screens that tempt and back to You, the true Lover of my soul.

Highway to Hell

Her house is a highway to the grave, leading down to the chambers of death.—Proverbs 7:27

S olomon knew a thing or two about the power of women. The wisest man in the world, full of strength and confidence, was completely brought down by seduction. If it could happen to him, it can happen to any of us. Seven hundred wives, three hundred concubines. He didn't stumble into that life. He walked deliberately down the highway, one compromise at a time, until he couldn't find his way back.

This isn't gentle advice. This is a warning sign on the edge of a cliff.

I was eight years old, sitting on Grandma's porch in rural Georgia, when she first read Proverbs 7 to me. Not the nice parts of Proverbs—the hard chapter, the uncomfortable one. She read slowly, making sure I understood every word about the adulterous woman, the simple young man, the path that leads to death.

Then she did something I'll never forget. She made me carry a pocket Bible everywhere I went. Just in case, a girl at school tried to kiss me—then I would be ready —Grandma said I should pull out that little Bible and physically put it up to my lips!

At eight years old, I thought it was a crazy idea. My friends thought it was hilarious. But Grandma wasn't playing games. She was putting the fear of God in me and a healthy caution about flirting with girls before I was old enough to understand why I needed it.

Looking back now, I realize what she was doing. She saw Solomon's highway and knew how easy it was to get on it. One look becomes a thought. One thought becomes fantasy. One fantasy becomes a conversation. One conversation becomes a compromise. And suddenly you're on a road you never meant to travel, headed toward chambers of death you never intended to enter.

The naive don't know they're naive. That's what makes them vulnerable. They think they can handle it, control it, and stop whenever they want. They think they're different, stronger, smarter than everyone else who's gone down this road.

Solomon was the wisest man alive, and this highway still destroyed him. What makes you think you're immune?

Grandma knew something at eight years old that I needed protection from, something I wouldn't face for years. She knew the highway starts earlier than we think, and once you're on it, getting off is exponentially harder than never getting on. I also learned later that she had the context of realities in my family that she was fiercely fighting against to break generational strongholds.

So here's the warning Solomon gives and Grandma enforced: **Stay away from the highway.** Not "be careful on it" or "you can handle it." Stay off it entirely. Because her house—whether that's a person, a screen, a fantasy—is a highway to the grave.

Father, thank You for Grandma's wisdom. Give me that same fierce protection for myself and those I love. Keep me off highways that lead to death. When I'm tempted to think I'm wise enough to handle it, remind me of Solomon. Let me be fearful and wise enough to believe Your warnings.

An Awestruck Ruler

By me, kings reign, and rulers issue decrees that are just. —Proverbs 8:15

***W**hen was the last time you were simply in awe of God and His wonders?*

When I consider your heavens, the work of your fingers, the moon, and the stars, which you have set in place, what is humanity that you are mindful of them, human beings that you care for?... You made them rulers over the works of your hands; you put everything under their feet (Psalm 8:3-6 NIV).

Do you remember that moment of perspective, clarity, and peace for your soul? We serve a mighty and awesome God! It's in these moments we cry out, 'O Lord, our Lord, how majestic is your name in all the earth' (1). God created the universe, time, seasons, mountains, valleys, sunrises, sunsets, flowers, trees, birds, and herds. Then he made you! Then 'God blessed them and said to them, "Be fruitful and increase in number, fill the earth and subdue it. Rule...over every living creature" (Genesis 1:28).

It's a charge, a covenant commission, before the corruption of sin and death. It's a charge the Psalmist gives us today, echoed from the beginning. It's what we were made to do. We are given stewardship over what God has created, and He said, 'rule.' What an incredible trust that God has given to men and women. Just as we stand in awe of God and His works, it's an awesome work that God has given us to do stewarding the works of His hands. We are to steward and rule over what the Master has entrusted into our hands.

Take an inventory of all that's in your domain...

- **Relationships** of Family, Friends, Community, Church, Workplace

- **Resources** of Time, Talent, and Treasure

If it helps, begin writing down all that God has entrusted to your care. Look at the list in your mind or print and consider the impact. It's awesome and potentially overwhelming. Yet, it's what we were made for by God: to be Fruitful, Multiply, Subdue, and Rule!

We were designed to work within an order. It's an order in our priorities, perspective, and even the events of our day. Begin the day, today even, with an awe of God. Cry out in praise, 'O Lord, our Lord, how majestic is your name in all the earth.' Then, let the promises of God resonate deep in your mind and soul that God is 'mindful' and 'cares for you' even as you go about the business of your day.

When God directs, He provides a way. Let us maintain the practice and perspective of praise as we pursue the purposes of our work. Then you will rule and steward well what's been entrusted to your care.

We're quickly overwhelmed with the awe of work when we're not overwhelmed by the awe of God's work. Keep the latter, and the former will find its balance.

Father, I let praise rise from my heart and mouth, O Lord, our Lord, how majestic is Your name in all the earth—help me start each day overwhelmed by awe of You before I'm overwhelmed by the work You've given me. Remind me today that You are mindful of me and care for me as I rule and steward well what's been entrusted to my care.

Wisdom's Embrace

I love those who love me, and those who seek me find me. —Proverbs 8:17

I remember sitting with some dear friends on a warm August afternoon, we celebrated the homecoming of their newly adopted son (10 months) and daughter (22 months) from Ethiopia. They have a family of five kids, with their oldest son, Gabe (8), who was off with my son, Grady (8), conquering the world in the backfield. Gabe has two little sisters, two adorable, curly-haired twin girls who were also adopted from Ethiopia a few years ago. I love this family. As adoptive parents, the first few months are critical to help nurture a bond with Mom and Dad. Yet, a little boy (10 months), who they call *Brut,* nearly flew out of his mother's arms, reaching for me when he heard my voice and saw me nearby. I grabbed that boy, and we regarded one another. Then he lit up a huge smile that just made my month. I bonded with little Brut.

'I love those who love me.' The affections of your heart are undeniable, for you don't have to look very far to see what you embrace. The embrace of a little Ethiopia baby boy won my heart with his open arms and smile. Consider for a moment today what you embrace. You may embrace it with the affection of your time, talent, and treasure. Jesus teaches us, 'For where your treasure is there your heart will be also' (Matthew 6:21). The motives of the heart are difficult to discern. However, your actions reveal your motives, for your actions may be measured by your time, talent, and treasure.

What or who do you love that truly loves you back? Really! What or who can you truly embrace with your affections and ambition that truly loves your back? The desire for power can be taken from you. A position or promotion that you're seeking or have attained can be demoted or dismissed. Possessions only satisfy for a short time once their newness have worn off. Again, consider the commitments of your day and the goals of your affections. Will what you love be able to love you back?

Today, we can fully embrace a wisdom promise that as we seek, we will find. How interesting that we hear the same language spoken by Jesus (Matthew 7:7-11). We will always find wisdom in the measure that we seek. For in finding the embrace of wisdom, we find the very embrace of God. Awesome! 'For whoever finds me finds life and receives favor from the Lord' (8:35). Yet, a word of caution. There is another way that leads to destruction and heartache, 'all who hate me love death' 8:36.

As believers in Christ, sons, and daughters in the Father's love, we are free from death. We are free from condemnation and control (Romans 8:1,6,8,9). For when I am under the power of the sinful nature, there is only death. Instead, when I yield to the leadership of the Spirit, there is 'life and peace' (6). I wrote in the margin of my bible, *do you have death on you or life and peace?* Let us turn in pursuit of wisdom and relationship, for the Lord God will embrace us as we embrace Him and bless us with wisdom, love, and grace.

Embrace the love of God, who always will embrace you back.

Father, I reach for You today with the open arms—help me embrace what truly loves me back instead of chasing things that can be taken away. Let me find life and peace as I pursue wisdom, knowing that when I embrace You, You always embrace me back with love and grace.

Milestone 3: The Entrepreneurial Engine

When I was in college, navigating the complexities of business school, I was fueled by a profound desire to one day start my own business. The prospect of independence as a small business owner or entrepreneur was both daunting and exhilarating. The journey was a mix of thrill and challenge. Where does one even start? What kind of business would I want to run? How would I operate it? Am I even equipped for this kind of challenge? These questions, rather than intimidating me, sparked a fire within me.

All of a sudden, the questions mounted up like a backlog of doubt, representing my insecurity and lack of confidence. The dream felt simultaneously within reach and impossibly distant. I could envision the freedom and fulfillment of entrepreneurship, but the practical realities seemed daunting for a young man who had never signed the front of a paycheck.

However, something remarkable happened while I was studying for my business degree. As I began actively pursuing mentors who were already operating successful businesses, a plan slowly began to form. During that unique season of writing business plans and preparing to launch, I found myself surrounded by five specific mentors who, in their way, provided crucial counsel about what it took to launch and run a business.

These weren't just casual advisors—they were seasoned entrepreneurs who had walked the path I was hoping to travel. They helped me understand things I didn't even know I didn't know. They guided me through the practical elements of business planning while also addressing the mental and emotional preparation required for entrepreneurship. Each mentor brought a unique perspective, offering financial wisdom, operational insights, marketing strategies, leadership principles, and the spiritual foundation necessary for ethical business practices.

Even with this incredible support system, I was still held back by my lack of confidence and the courage actually to begin. The gap between preparation and action felt enormous. But something in the pursuit of wisdom from those who had walked before me began to prepare me in ways I couldn't have imagined. Their counsel didn't just fill knowledge gaps—it built the confidence I needed to take that first terrifying step. Their guidance was not just about business but also about life and leadership. It was a reassurance that I was not alone in this journey.

On October 1st, 1996, I walked down to the courthouse and got my business license. That afternoon, I began making phone calls to pursue opportunities and potential customers. It was both the most exhilarating and terrifying day of my professional life. Almost exactly one hundred days later, to the date, I received my first contract and my first check. That moment launched what would become a fifteen-year entrepreneurial journey as a small business owner.

Looking back on those years, my entrepreneurship was founded on more than just business acumen or market opportunity. It was rooted in pursuing the Lord and being obedient to stewarding who I am as a leader and entrepreneur. The foundation was both spiritual and practical.

But as I reflect on all those years—the successes, failures, lessons learned, and relationships built—what sustained me through the inevitable challenges was the pursuit of wisdom and the ongoing counsel of mentors along the way. Seeking wise counsel wasn't just what got me started; it's what allowed me to be sustained as a business owner through every season.

The entrepreneurial engine that drove those fifteen years wasn't just ambition or opportunity—it was wisdom actively pursued and faithfully applied. This wisdom, gained through experience and the guidance of mentors, was the light that guided me through the darkest of times and the beacon that led me to success.

Character of the Craftsman

Then, I was the craftsman at his side; I was filled with delight day after day, rejoicing always in his presence.
—Proverbs 8:30

Listen to old Solomon personify wisdom as the Craftsman during the account of creation. The author of wisdom, the Creator, established the foundations of the earth and brought life, order, and whimsically whispered sunrises and sunsets. We bask under the glow of creation for uncounted dawns and dusks. Do you not also find yourself 'filled with delight' and 'rejoicing always in his presence?' Whether standing on vistas, listening to the crash of the waves on the shore, or hearing the birds in a quiet corner of a park in the city, does not something in your soul settle? Now consider the crown of creation.... you... others... loved ones in your life, friends, neighbors, co-workers.

The Genesis 1 account reveals the Triune God at work in creation: "In the beginning God created the heavens and the earth," with the "Spirit of God hovering over the waters, bringing order from chaos," and "through the Word, all things were made." The same Triune God—the Creator of the universe and Craftsman of wisdom—is your companion no matter where you are on your journey. In every circumstance, he offers comfort and counsel.

Whatever project currently has your attention, invite the Craftsman to collaborate alongside you. Allow him to impart ideas that have been tested and proven faithful. Let the Craftsman shape your thinking in ways that will protect your attitudes, words, and actions. Yet, you may need to slow your pace, pause in your steps, and ask without doubt; then, like any good apprentice, be patient for the Master's instruction, guidance, and full attention.

We are in the midst of the project. It has been going on since the creation of the world. Our creation. We are the project. God is our Creator, and wisdom is the Craftsman working and shaping us into the people of God. Sons and Daughters. Let us yield to the Craftsman's hand today. Notice when you see his hand at work, forming and shaping. Please take a moment to see his progress, then capture a vision for the work yet to be done by the Master. How has the Craftsman shaped you? What work is yet to be completed?

As you yield under his hand, your soul will be filled 'with delight day after day, rejoicing always in his presence.' When we lose our delight and our joy, then our formation slows. Delight and joy are the grace that is the lifeblood of your spiritual formation.

Let us consider the projects we have undertaken. Have they robbed us of our delight and joy? Let us yield those to the Craftsman for His inspection and oversight. Let us lay down or complete what is secondary, then take hold of his great project, the building of his kingdom, and for his glory displayed in and through our lives for eternity. Let that start today, and today, you will find delight and joy in his presence.

Father, you are the Master Craftsman, I yield to Your shaping hands today—slow my pace so I can be patient for Your instruction and see the work You're doing in me. Help me lay down what's secondary to take hold of Your best work. Fill my soul with delight today as I enjoy working alongside You.

Listen Intently

Now then, my sons, listen to me; blessed are those who keep my ways. —*Proverbs 8:32*

I love watching my Golden Retrievers when I pull out a bone. In an instant, their playful distraction vanishes, and I have their complete, undivided attention. They hang on my every word and gesture, ears perked forward, eyes locked on mine, bodies trembling with anticipation. They comply instantly with my commands because they know their prize awaits. Dogs possess this remarkable ability to focus intently on what their appetites truly crave.

James 1:22-25 reveals a similar pattern for those pursuing wisdom. We're charged to listen intently as a pathway toward the blessed life—paying careful attention to words of wisdom and not forgetting what we've heard. Like my eager retrievers, we need to crave wisdom with that same intense focus and expectation.

Yet here's our challenge: What noise keeps us from listening? The ancient wisdom reminds us that God gave us two ears and one mouth for a reason. Too often, my own words get in the way of listening well. Internal chatter, rehearsed responses, and the urgent need to be heard all compete with our ability to truly listen. James calls us to be "quick to listen, slow to speak, and slow to become angry"—a discipline that requires intentional practice in our noisy world.

Consider the barriers that prevent us from listening intently. Sometimes, it's the relentless pace of modern life, with notifications constantly demanding our attention. At other times, it's our own pride, assuming we already know what needs to be said. Fear can also deafen us—we're afraid we might hear something that requires uncomfortable change. Even past disappointments can close our ears; when we've been hurt by poor counsel before, we become skeptical of all guidance.

Solomon's invitation comes as a loving father speaking to his children: "Listen to me." It's not the harsh demand of an impatient authority figure but the tender appeal of someone who genuinely wants what's best for us. He promises that those who keep his ways will be blessed—not because the path is always easy, but because wisdom leads to life in its most whole form.

This requires us to meditate on the Lord's way. Take time to examine your current path—where have your choices led you? Then look up to see if your direction is drawing you closer to God or pulling you away from Him. The ways of the Lord are characterized by wisdom, faith, and love. When we set our hearts in pursuit of these qualities, we position ourselves to receive His guidance.

What is the way of the Lord for you today? How is He leading you in your relationships, your work, and your character development? What specific words is He speaking that you need to hear? It could be encouragement for a weary heart, correction for a wayward habit, or direction for an important decision.

The beautiful promise embedded in this passage is that God desires to communicate with His children. Like a loving father, He speaks counsel, direction, and life over us. But we must learn to listen intently, filtering out the noise and distractions that compete for our attention.

Father, quiet every noise competing for my attention so I can listen to You with the eager focus waiting for your leading. Help me crave Your wisdom more than anything else, give me ears that truly listen and a heart ready to obey what I hear.

Simple Ways

Leave your simple ways, and you will live; walk in the way of understanding. —Proverbs 9:6

I n a world of complexity, the simple has an attraction. Working with leaders, I have found that you often have to understand complexity to gain access to its simplicity. Look at any good brand promise or vision statement from an organization, and you'll find plenty of complexity behind its formation. Listen to the pithy wisdom of an older sage who shares a simple principle, yet there's a lifetime of history and a cost to his pain. Karl Barth, the noted theologian who wrote volumes and lectured for decades on all matters of 'truth' of the Christian faith, was asked at the end of his days before an Ivy League audience to explain salvation. He answered, 'Jesus loves me; this I know for the Bible tells me so.' There is a genius of understanding to find simplicity in a world of complexity. As we mature in wisdom, insight, and knowledge, heed the counsel of the proverb to 'leave your simple ways and live.'

As Paul wrote, 'When I was a child, I talked like a child, I thought like a child, I reasoned like a child. When I became a man, I put the ways of childhood behind me (1 Corinthians 13:11). We are called to a life of maturity in Christ. To 'walk in the way of understanding,' we should consider our childish or foolish thinking and behavior. If you find it difficult to see childish tendencies in your actions and attitudes, I encourage, rather challenge, you to a learning exercise. *Spend time with some children.* Watch and learn from them. Their laughter and curiosity may inspire and spark some new energy and enthusiasm in you. They'll also give you some funny stories to tell. During your time with a child, you may observe some of their 'foolish' tendencies. You may notice a slight irritation rise within you. You may see some of their actions and attitudes still reflected within you, yet we do a better job of masking our motives. Notice as their actions escalate without some boundaries or discipline, you find yourself like Solomon, responding with 'forsake the foolishness and live' (KJV).

Regarding kids, let us have the same attitude and access as Jesus as he called, 'Let the little children come to me and do not hinder them, for to such belongs the kingdom of heaven' (Matthew 19:14). For it is through the innocence of childlike faith that we gain access to our heavenly Father who loves and adores us as sons and daughters. *Let us never lose the grace of a simple faith, for* it is in the presence of the Lord that we find all wisdom, insight, and understanding.

Build and cultivate a simple faith, but consider your 'simple ways' (NIV) and 'forsake the foolish' (KJV) in your life. If your foolish choices have yielded a life of pain and consequence, come quickly to the Lord and receive grace and forgiveness. Let God comfort, heal, and restore you. Now, begin the journey today away from those 'foolish' habits and 'walk in the way of understanding' and then 'you will live.' If you have complexities, ask the Lord for wisdom; he will grant you simplicity amid the complexity. As you ask, the Lord will provide, then receive the promise that 'you are wise, your wisdom will reward you' (9:12). Embrace, enjoy, and share the reward today of simple faith and wisdom while turning from simple ways.

Father, help me leave foolish ways behind while keeping child-like faith that gives me access to You. Heal where my simple ways caused pain, and walk me into understanding that leads to life. Grant me wisdom to find Your simplicity in life's complexity.

Response to Rebuke

Do not rebuke a mocker, or he will hate you; rebuke a wise man, and he will love you. Instruct a wise man, and he will be wiser still; teach a righteous man, and he will add to his learning. —Proverbs 9:8-9

D o you want to be wise? How far are you willing to go to gain wisdom? These words reveal the depths you may have to go to gain wisdom. It's a risk yet with great reward.

Consider the simplicity of the words love and hate; they are perplexing in their implications. Now think of a person you know for each, and it invokes quite an emotion for those individuals. Do not underestimate the power and reality of both. We live in a world of love and hate. Lives, families, friendships, businesses, churches, and institutions rise and fall every day from these two realities. They invite or unlock a passion in our lives for building up or tearing down. Let us be discerning of the character of both wise and foolish in our lives.

There are so many complexities to working with people. Yet, we are given a key indicator of the future in the response to a rebuke. These words are not a permission slip to go around exhorting everyone in our lives. Let us mind Jesus' words: 'First take the plank out of your eye, and then you will see clearly to remove the speck from your brother's eye' (Matthew 7:5). It's from a humble and clean heart that we would even approach another with words of correction. It also implies some level of relationship, history, and context to the situation. It also requires a level of permission to offer an observation, counsel, or correction. One might say, 'Given our time together, I've observed something in your life that I would like to discuss with your permission either now or another time when you are ready.' Permission opens the door of the heart and mind for a change. Exhortation or a rebuke is a form of encouragement. The only reason you share your concern is because you love that person. A rebuke shared under compulsion or hate will certainly invoke a response of hate. Let us be wise in the rebuke that we come with pure motives of genuine love.

Response to a rebuke reveals respect for authority. Broken or abused authority in the past, a person will always reveal himself in the present. A rebuke often comes right to the heart of that pain, and the response may have nothing to do with the rebuke, the situation, or the context of the relationship. It may reveal an unresolved hurt that needs healing, as well as grace and mercy. These painful authority figures are often linked to your family of origin, bosses, spiritual leaders, mentors, or even broken friendships. A soul tie that was given to another in your past. We all share a past marked by some level of brokenness, and we need to offer an abundance of grace to one another.

A rebuke is a risk - to destroy or to build. It reveals a level of maturity despite past hurts, authority challenges, and idiotic notions. Solomon writes earlier in the passage, 'Leave your simple ways, and you will live' (9:6). A pathway to wisdom is a progression of maturity. A rebuke shows where we are on the path: fools or wise revealed in hate or love. There is great joy in a response of love because it demonstrates maturity and readiness for more. 'Instruct...wiser still.' 'Teach...he will learn.' It's a developmental pathway for those open to rebuke. It certainly doesn't feel good, but it's a blessing for those who will receive it. 'Let a righteous man strike me---it is a kindness; let him rebuke me- it is oil on my head. My head will not refuse it (Psalm 141:5).' Let us not be easily offended today by the correction of another, even if it's in the most unlikely direction.

We quickly ask for wisdom, yet the means of wisdom are not always in the easiest of the ways. Just as cautioning yourself to pray for patience, you will undoubtedly face a trial that will hopefully help develop your patience. Like a good father, God's means of imparting wisdom are not limited. You ask, and He gives generously to all without finding fault (James 1). Yet, today, it may come through a rebuke. Will you respond in hate or love? If you love, then you are on the pathway to maturity, completeness, and not lacking anything. Then, you are ready for more that the Lord has in store for you. As you love a rebuke, remember the significant risk your friend has taken in approaching you. Be grateful. Thank them for their kindness, and your relationship will continue to grow.

Father, prepare my heart today for any admonishment or exhortation. Let me not be quickly offended, but receive the gift of correction. Remove hate from my heart. Heal my broken places and pieces from past hurts. Remove the plank in my eye so I can see. Let me be a great lover of people and wisdom as you are to me.

Walking Securely

Whoever walks in integrity walks securely, but whoever takes crooked paths will be found out.—Proverbs 10:9

I've heard it said that being principled is doing what's right even when no one is watching. But there's more to it than that—**integrity doesn't just protect your character; it protects your life.**

My pastor in Georgia told a story about going to Golden Corral for lunch with his family. His son was one year over the age limit for a child's lunch price, but he thought, "He's small for his age. What harm would there be in saving some money?"

Then conviction hit: Is my character worth only $4.99? What message am I sending to my kids? Do I want them to believe it's okay to lie when it saves you a few bucks? He decided his integrity wasn't for sale—not even at a buffet discount.

That's what Solomon means by "walking securely." When you walk in integrity, you're not constantly looking over your shoulder. You're not afraid of being exposed because there's nothing to hide. You sleep well. You face people confidently. You walk securely.

But **whoever takes crooked paths will be found out.**

Every mother knows when her child is up to no good. It's an instinct born from relationship—she knows her child's voice, their patterns, the tell-tale silence that means trouble. When she calls out, "What are you doing in there?" she already knows. The question isn't for her information; it's an invitation for the child to come clean.

Moms don't play "gotcha" to shame their kids; they ask questions to teach them integrity. The goal isn't exposure for exposure's sake. It's teaching children that hiding in shame is more exhausting than walking in honesty. Those crooked paths lead to anxiety, but integrity leads to security.

Here's the truth we learn as children but forget as adults: **you can't hide forever.**

You will be found out. Not necessarily by public exposure, but by the internal weight of living dishonestly. The sleepless nights. The constant vigilance. The fear that someone will discover what you're hiding.

Crooked paths feel secure in the moment but lead to exhaustion and anxiety. Straight paths might feel vulnerable, but they lead to the security and peace of having nothing to hide.

God isn't waiting to catch you doing something wrong so He can punish you. Like a good mother, He's inviting you to take responsibility. To do the right thing even when no one's watching. To walk in the light instead of hiding in shadows.

Whatever path you're on today, consider where it leads. Are you compromising in small ways that feel harmless—like a $4.99 lunch lie? Are you taking crooked shortcuts, thinking no one will know?

Taking responsibility and doing the right thing even when no one is looking—that's the wisdom of walking securely. Not hiding. Not waiting to be found out. Just walking honestly, openly, with nothing to fear.

Father, I want to walk securely in integrity, not anxiously on crooked paths waiting to be found out. Thank You for inviting me out of hiding into the light—not to shame me but to teach me the security that comes from having nothing to hide.

Diligent Discipline

He who heeds discipline shows the way to life,
but whoever ignores correction leads others astray.
—Proverbs 10:17

W hat are we modeling in our work, and to whom?

There may be no greater pain caused in one's life than to realize our actions have caused another to be led astray. We should be cautious not to underestimate our value and influence in others' lives, starting with our families, friendships, and broader circles. How many men who have once stood their post as husbands and fathers abandoned their responsibilities, leaving a family to fend for themselves? How long does it take to mend the hurt from another's broken promises or foolish choices? We need to consider how well we heed discipline.

We need to be disciplined in our disciplines. Yet, we are called back to the center again today. However far afield we might have strayed, we have a choice to heed discipline. A simple choice of responsibility for what has been entrusted to you today. It requires work, sacrifice, time, and energy to do the right thing. *What are the right things you need to do today? And how do you do them right?*

Every day, there are distractions from our work and our disciplines; we could likely busy ourselves with more interesting, appealing, or even fulfilling things in the moment. 'Lazy hands make a man poor, but diligent hands bring wealth' (10:4). What task is before you today that requires not only discipline but *diligent discipline*? In your character of diligence, there will be a return for your work. The task of discipline also yields a return. A task accomplished yields a sense of fulfillment, indicating a job well done. Yet, could it be more fulfilling than the fruit of your labor that your discipline 'shows the way to life.' That's a powerful principle.

Heeding the discipline gives life to those who matter most. If I become lazy in my work, it may set a precedent and model for my wife and children that could cause them to stumble and lose their way. Let us be reminded that our diligent discipline leads others to the path of life. I pray I do not neglect my responsibilities only to see the reality of the proverbs, thus leading others astray down a destructive path.

Let's renew our vision to the nobility of work that leads to the path of life today for ourselves and those in our lives by pressing into the task of the day with diligence.

Father, give me strength today for the task you have laid before me. Thank you for your work. Let me honor with every thought, word, and deed throughout the day. Grant me the grace to stay steady on the path of life, no matter the difficulty of the task before me today.

Watch Your Mouth

———◄◆►———

The mouth of the righteous is a fountain of life,
but violence overwhelms the mouth of the wicked.
—Proverbs 10:11

Recently, a friend and business owner shared with me that he had a desire to share the Lord in some way through every conversation. What a noble goal! Yet, there were days that he would not speak a word of life into any conversation. As an engineer, he felt challenged to use his words in a way that honored the Lord in every encounter. My challenge to him was to take a notepad, draw two columns, and write down the names of people that you talked with throughout your day. Then, in the second column, write down how you spoke truth, encouragement, or a redemption story. The exercise brings awareness of relationships, focuses your time, and reveals the attitude of your heart and the words you share. What an inspiring goal from my friend to honor the Lord through every conversation.

Watch your mouth, lips, and tongue, for your words bring life or destruction. Consider the way and words you speak that either represent the wise or the fool. Solomon wrote with such repetition in this passage on the influence and impact of our mouth for life or violent tearing down. Read and reflect on the words of Proverbs 10 on the effects of your words.

- For the Wise - the foundation of life (11), discerning (12), knowledge (13), honesty (18), restraint (19), choice silver (20) nourish many (21), wisdom (31), what is fitting (32).

- For the fool - chattering (8)(10), violence (11), rod on the back (12), ruin (13), slander (18), sin (19), little value (20), lack of judgment (21), perverse (31)(32).

Who will you be today? The fool or the wise? *Measure your words by the attitude of your heart and thoughts in your mind.* As you reflect on the attributes above, begin writing down the names of people in your life with whom you will speak today or this week. Measure your words by planning your speech for wisdom. Take on the attitude of the wise so that you will represent the benefits of the wise. For that will be a blessing to the listener and the hearer.

Many of us have heard messages and teachings on 'taming the tongue' (James 3:8-12). We must listen to a caution of our speech balanced with a heart of love, or our words and actions are like a 'clanging cymbal' (1 Corinthians 13:1). As believers in Christ, filled with His Spirit, we should desire our words and speech to be 'for their strengthening, encouragement, and comfort" (14:3). When we speak let it be words of hope for the UnChristian and edification for the believers to 'build up the church' (14:12). For one day, maybe sooner than we think, 'every tongue will confess that Jesus Christ is Lord' (Philippians 2:11). Let us guard our tongues, speak with attitudes and actions of love, sharing words that bring hope and courage and praise and honor to the one worthy of all glory. For from the Lord and his righteousness, he has spoken over you a 'fountain of life' by forgiveness, grace, and mercy. Let us go and do the same today.

Father, make my mouth a fountain of life today—let every conversation honor You and speak hope, encouragement, and truth to those I encounter. Guard my tongue from chattering, slander, and violence. Help me measure my words before I speak them, building up instead of tearing down.

Prospect of Joy

The prospect of the righteous is joy, but the hopes of the wicked come to nothing. —Proverbs 10:28.

I n Colorado, there is a well-known gambling town located west of Colorado Springs known as Cripple Creek. One hundred years ago, it was better known as a mining town. It's known as the biggest gold rush, both *Boom and Bust,* in United States history. In today's economy, billions of dollars worth of gold were shipped from its mines. Recently, I hiked with a small band of brothers to an 11,000-foot mountain that overlooks America's first scenic highway, which all US Presidents traveled on from the 1920s to the 1970s. What a memorable moment to consider what it would have been like to live and work in that community during the time of the Boom. Many of us today have experienced seasons of Booms and Busts. It's the best and worst of times.

Consider the season and the prospect of your work today. Is it a boom or a bust season? In either situation, you're still prospecting for the next gold strike. You could be mining your gold knowing that vein will end one day, or you're still searching. The venture before you today sets your ambition to solve a problem, meet a goal, or capitalize on the next opportunity. When you put your mind and heart to the work, it's exciting and compelling. No doubt there are challenges.

Some detours may distract you and lead you down the wrong tunnel. Yet, you are still prospecting! Consider the goal of your find. Miners would shout 'Yureka!' when they chip away the last rock and find the mother lode. Consider the goal of your pursuit today. What are your prospects for today? Will you know success when you see it?

Reflect on this promise, 'Hope does not disappoint us, because God has poured out his love into our hearts by the Holy Spirit, whom he has given us' (Romans 5:5). Could it be that the prospect of your pursuit is joy? Let us not be like the wicked whose 'hopes...come to nothing.' I pity the miners of old who worked their claim only to find nothing right next to the mine that carried the mother lode. Again, consider the goal of your prospecting today. Will the riches you see in times of Boom give you fulfillment only to have it lost in times of Bust? Look deeper into the promises of God today.

We are called to rejoice! Rejoice! God is forming you from the inside out. He is forming you through suffering, perseverance, and character, which leads to hope that does not disappoint (Romans 5:3-5). Work today with diligence on the prospects before you. Yet, do so, having already claimed what your heart desires. *Joy!* God has a mother lode found in Jesus Christ.

Your work today is to believe (John 6:29). Will you believe the promise of God that he has poured out his love to you? He has hope that will never disappoint (Romans 5:7). Consider your commitments, ambitions, and your prospects today. Determine in your heart if you have not already found the gold your heart seeks.

Father, help me stop prospecting for gold that disappears in the bust and start claiming the joy that's already mine in Christ. Let me work diligently today, form me through every boom and bust, knowing my true prospect is joy that never disappoints.

Generous Refreshment

A generous person will prosper; whoever refreshes others will be refreshed.—Proverbs 11:25

I'm exhausted. The tank is empty. Every leadership book tells me to practice self-care, set boundaries, and fill my own cup first. And honestly, part of me wants to close the door, turn off my phone, and focus on me for a while.

But here's what I've discovered through the decades of practicing this proverb: **the way of refreshment comes through being a refreshment for others.**

It's counterintuitive. It doesn't make sense to our self-preservation instincts. When you're running on fumes, the last thing logic tells you to do is give more away. Yet there's this kingdom principle that defies human reasoning: as we refresh others, we ourselves are refreshed.

I'm not talking about giving to the point of burnout—there's no wisdom in that. I'm not suggesting you ignore chronic fatigue or sacrifice your health on the altar of endless service. **Wisdom requires balance.**

But here's the tension: we can become so focused on filling ourselves up that we become stagnant pools instead of flowing rivers. A pond that only collects eventually grows algae and dies. A river that continually gives and receives stays fresh, alive, vital.

Think about the people who've been generous to you. Not just with money, but with time, attention, and encouragement. That friend who sent a text at exactly the right moment. The mentor who made time when they didn't have time. The person who noticed you were struggling and did something about it.

What did their generosity do for you? It lifted you. Encouraged you. Reminded you that you weren't alone. And here's the mystery: when you ask them about it, they often say giving to you blessed them more than it cost them.

That's the phenomenon of generosity—in giving away, we receive back. Not always from the same person, not always in the same way, but the Father fills our cups again and again as we pour out for others.

I'm learning this isn't about grand gestures. It's about a generous mindset. A few minutes today to send an encouraging word. A small act of service that interrupts your schedule but makes someone's day. Noticing who needs refreshment and choosing to be the river, rather than the stagnant pool.

Who in your life needs refreshment today? Not this month, not this week—today. Who needs to hear they matter, they're doing better than they think, they're not alone? It might take five minutes. It might be the best moment of their day.

Here's what happens when you do it, even from a place of exhaustion: something shifts in your soul. The act of looking beyond yourself, of focusing on another's need instead of your own, lifts the weight. Not because you've solved all your problems, but because you've participated in something bigger than yourself. There's power in your weakness (2 Corinthians 12:10).

The generous person prospers—not always financially, but always spiritually. When you refresh others, you are refreshed. That's not a nice idea. That's a kingdom principle. So today, even if you're tired—be the river. Let generosity flow through you. Watch what God does in return.

Father, I'm tired, but I don't want to be stagnant. Make me a river of Your generosity. Show me who needs refreshment today. Give me eyes to see beyond my own needs. As I pour out, fill me back up. Let me discover the mystery of being refreshed by refreshing others. Make me generous like You.

Seek Righteousness

Whoever trusts in his riches will fall, but the righteous will thrive like a green leaf. —Proverbs 11:28

So often, I sit with men who say, 'I don't hear from God.' They experience a quiet frustration from the disconnect in their souls. Yet, in their confession, they acknowledge a deep longing to know God and hear his voice. For if we are all honest, we all have questions to be answered, an insecurity that needs healing, sin to be cleansed, and a desire for the love of the Father. If these needs and desires are not fulfilled, then we attempt to do so by our means only to remain an empty cup.

If you sense the ache of an unsettled soul, quiet yourself before the Lord this day. Lay down your burdens, confess your sins, and give your desires. For in doing so, you open yourself to a renewed mind and restored soul. Let your mind and heart be washed in the word. Take hold of God's promises that speak truth over any lies that govern your thoughts.

Consider the object of your trust today. How much do you trust in your resources above trusting in the Lord? For trust in your own 'riches' creates an anxiety or worry that cripples you in a form of fear. It cripples your faith from listening and hearing the voice of the Spirit who wants to speak to you today. Free yourself from trust in your abilities, connections, and reputation. Let your character be known as one who trusts in the Lord above anything else.

'Seek first his kingdom and righteousness, and all these things will be given to you as well' Matthew 6:33. Seek first... Will you? Will you believe today that he has resources beyond your own? Your access to those resources comes by setting your love, service, and faith in the Lord. It's his righteousness that makes us right above our own ability to do so. It's his kingdom that's so much more important than our own.

When we are bound by worry, anxiety, and fear, it reveals the object of our trust. Confess these things that would cripple your faith. In doing so, you open up the communication lines for the voice of God in your life. In doing so, your soul will move from surviving to thriving. God's heart for you is to thrive. 'All these things will be added to you,' that's a promise. Believe it! Consider how you may seek his righteousness by faith today. Look closely at the instruction from Proverbs 11; there are 16 verses regarding the righteous life. Let the word of the Lord guide you in a virtuous life today.

Quiet your busy mind and heart. Clean out the clutter of a crippled soul. Rest and restore before the Lord today. He wants to speak to you. Listen, learn, then seek. He's waiting...

Father, I confess I've been trusting my own resources more than You—quiet my anxious soul so I can hear Your voice. Help me seek Your kingdom first today, believing thriving comes from trusting You, not my abilities. Clean out the clutter; I'm ready to listen and rest in You.

Milestone 4: Love Of A Father

I can't think of a time in my life when I was more overwhelmed with love—a love I didn't even know I had the capacity for—than when I saw my first baby girl, Ellie. Being a dad of daughters unlocks something deep inside a man: the desire to fight, the desire to protect, the desire to provide, and the desire to be present. I never felt that more powerfully than when I became the father of Ellie, Bethany, and Grady.

The theme of having the capacity to love deeply indeed flows from my love of God and was modeled in my relationship with Cari, but there's something uniquely special about being a dad. Even with all the challenges of growing up and seeing mixed messages about what love and true love meant from my family, all I knew was that I was crazy about my kids. I felt such a deep desire to love them well.

But therein lies the challenge that led me to an almost desperate point: How do I love my kids well? How do I not mess them up? How do I help them face the challenges that the world brings their way? How do I become the dad they need me to be to help prepare them for the life ahead?

This desperate pursuit of wanting to be a good dad put me on my knees before God, seeking wisdom like never before. As we explore throughout this journey, wisdom is a free commodity. The ability to pursue wisdom is something God gives generously, and James 1:5 reminds us that He gives it without finding fault. I knew I needed wisdom more than ever as a dad.

How do I be a father to daughters? With no sisters, I had never even seen what it looked like to raise girls. All I had was my brother as a model for what it looked like to grow up in an environment with other boys. Now I had little girls looking at me, interested in dress-up, wanting help fixing their hair, eager for tea parties. Where do I even begin as their dad?

More importantly, how do I navigate their hearts and emotions through early school days, junior high, high school, and their journey into becoming young adults? The complexity of raising a son and daughters in today's world has felt overwhelming at times.

But there's nothing that motivated me more to pursue wisdom than wanting to be the dad my kids needed. I discovered that while there's no such thing as a perfect dad, the pursuit of wisdom opens our hearts to love deeper while also providing the insight, discernment, and guidance necessary to raise our children well.

This milestone taught me that fatherhood isn't just about providing and protecting—it's about pursuing wisdom daily. Every challenge my children faced became an opportunity for me to seek God's guidance. Every question they asked, every tear they shed, and every celebration they experienced drove me deeper into prayer and Scripture.

The love of a father, I learned, is best expressed not through perfection but through the humble pursuit of wisdom. In seeking to love my children well, I discovered dimensions of God's love I had never known before.

Roots

A man cannot be established through wickedness, but the righteous cannot be uprooted. —*Proverbs 12:3*

W e had a problem buying our first home in Georgia. It was a little farmhouse sitting on 2 acres. The appraisal revealed a higher value for the land than for the buildings. We fell in love with that little 1,200 sq ft fixer-upper, not so much for the house, but for the trees. There were two 150-year-old oak trees on the property that defined it. For nearly nine years, we lived under those oaks. Proverbs 12:3 reflects the words from Isaiah 61:3: 'They will be called oaks of righteousness, a planting of the Lord for the display of his splendor.'

Think of the people that you most admire, search out and heed their counsel, and with whom you enjoy spending time. Who are those you value most? Likely they are those who are established, consistent, and faithful regardless of life's challenges. That doesn't mean they have not seen hardship; people who are oaks have stood firm in the storms. They have the character of steadfastness and consistency.

God wants His people to be deeply rooted through their walk with him and in the understanding and application of his word. The concept and context of developing roots have little to do with geography. While it might be true for some (my great uncle was in the same church for over 60 years and was known as an oak in his church and community), Jesus commissions us to 'Go' into all the world (Matthew 28:18-20). We are his witnesses, starting right where we are today (Acts 1:8), then stepping out. *He wants to establish our roots deep relationally in Him, on his promises, and with his people.* 'Blessed is the man who trusts in the Lord, whose confidence is in him. He will be like a tree planted by the water that sends out its roots by the stream (Jeremiah 17:7-8).

Let us examine our hearts today and confess what is wicked and unrighteous. Such things rot our root structure and destabilize our ability to withstand the storm. Let us be wise regarding temptation towards anything that does not reflect his righteousness. Let us walk today in the confidence that we are righteous in Christ, and he wants to establish his people as witnesses in our families, schools, workplaces, communities, churches, and beyond. Let us dwell in the Lord's presence and meditate on his promises (Joshua 1:8)(Psalm 1:1-3) (James 1:22-25). For in him, 'the righteous cannot be uprooted.'

Father, I confess my sins and come under Your righteousness—establish me as an oak that cannot be uprooted. Sanctify me in Your presence and renew my mind with Your promises so my roots grow deep in You. Let me go into the world today rooted in Your righteousness for Your glory, not my own.

Good Fruit

*From the fruit of his lips, a man is filled with good
things as surely as the work of his hands rewards him.*
—Proverbs 12:14

F ruit is God's dessert for his people. Sweet and satisfying to nourish
the body and soul. When I enjoy eating fruit, I often think of the
wedding feast in heaven that is being prepared for the church. I can only
imagine the reception, the celebration, and the food on the table. There
will be mountains of fruit filled with color, perfectly ripened, sweet to
the taste. Oh, how I love fruit.

The scriptures are filled with metaphoric language of fruit. Biblically
speaking, fruit from men comes from the heart. *A good heart begets good
fruit. An evil heart begets bad fruit.* Jesus gives us much to chew on from
John 15 regarding fruit. The key is the source. Do we abide in the vine
of God's grace and forgiveness found in Christ?

Today's proverb is written in plain language to confirm the same truth.
The words of a man's mouth and his actions reveal the attitude and
ambition of his heart and mind. Your words and actions will either betray
you or validate the good intentions you hold. When you meditate on the
proverb, 'good things' and 'reward' are the focus.

We are wired and destined for reward. We are made to produce. It's by
design what we are made to do (Genesis 1:28). We are made to work, and
what we create will yield a reward. It's God's blessing to us, and he calls
it good. Yet, a Day is coming when our work will be tested, and we will
be rewarded for its quality (Matthew 25:29, 1 Corinthians 3:8, 14). It's

bothersome and sobering to consider that your words and work today will echo in eternity.

Consider the works of your hands today, measure your words, consider your thoughts, and consecrate your heart to the Lord. Heed the counsel of the proverbs, fill your mouth with good things. Let your lips speak the truth in love, words of wisdom for a difficult challenge, encouragement to someone who has none, or comfort for the hurting. Saturate your mind and heart with the words of God that they will flow from your lips and hands.

For the good things that come forth will bring you a reward not only for today but also for the Day to Come. It's a covenant that God wants to bless his people with good things and reward those who earnestly seek him. When you seek him, you will find him, and He will fill you with such good fruits (Galatians 5:22-23). As you abide in Him, you become God's fruit; it's what *is sweet to those you meet.*

Father, fill my heart with Your goodness so the fruit of my lips and hands brings life to everyone I meet today. Let me abide so deeply in You that Your Spirit's fruit flows naturally from me—love, joy, peace, patience, kindness, goodness, faithfulness, gentleness, and self-control.

On the Edge of Quitting

*From the fruit of his lips, a man is filled with good
things as surely as the work of his hands rewards him.*
—*Proverbs 12:14*

F rustration was written all over his face. My eighteen-year-old son, Grady, was hunched over the engine bay of his car, attempting to change spark plugs for the first time. What should have been a straightforward job had turned into a mechanical nightmare. Bolts wouldn't turn. His hands couldn't reach the back plugs. The socket wrench kept slipping.

"This is impossible," he muttered, knuckles scraped, and patience wearing thin. For a young man just learning his way around engines, the gap between YouTube tutorials and actual mechanical reality felt overwhelming. Everything looked easy on the screen. Nothing was easy under the hood.

But he didn't quit. He adjusted his approach, found different tools, contorted his body into uncomfortable angles, and kept working. Two hours later—sweaty, grease-stained, but victorious—he fired up the engine. It purred. The roughness was gone. He'd done it.

The smile on his face said everything. That hard-earned satisfaction of persevering through frustration and completing difficult work. "I actually did it," he said, half-surprised, completely proud. In that moment, I saw a boy becoming a man through the simple act of refusing to give up.

What words will I say that will reveal the reward of my work?

Good things often come through the most challenging moments. Challenging moments present the greatest temptation for us to give up. It's been said that great moments come from great opportunities. Great opportunities are rarely handed to you. As a friend and mentor shared with me this week, leaders must regularly slog through the swamp to reach the mountaintop.

Mountain top moments are a great reward. It's a celebration for you and those with you, even from the victorious mountaintop of changing spark plugs for the first time. The victory is found in endurance and the enjoyment of the fruit of reward.

As you face your challenge today, whether you're working on your exercise or dealing with the daily grind, take a moment to think about your reward. **Where are you heading?** Whether you are on a 3-day or 3-year project, what awaits you at the finish? Some say it's the gain, yet for most, we find joy and satisfaction in completed work. Your smile reveals the fruit of your work.

If you're in the midst of good or even great work, the road is likely long. For greater vision, there is often a greater need for endurance. As you're on the slow, steady march to where you're going, consider how you're truly doing. The destination matters little if character has been compromised along the way.

Whether your role is that of a leader or a follower, you have an incredible opportunity to influence the reward of your work simply by your attitude and effort along the way. Whether you are managing the mundane or summiting the mountain top, prepare your heart and mind for what's refreshed and renewed in God's good prepared for you. Then the good fruit of your words and the good reward of work will follow.

Father, give me perseverance to work through frustration instead of quitting when things get hard. Let the fruit of my lips encourage others and the work of my hands bring satisfaction that points back to You.

Antidote to Anxiety

An anxious heart weighs a man down, but a kind word cheers him up. —Proverbs 12:25

T he alarm goes off too early. Before your feet hit the floor, your mind is already racing through the impossible deadlines waiting at the office. The project was due yesterday. The presentation you haven't finished. The emails are stacking up in your inbox like an avalanche you'll never dig out from under. Your to-do list has a to-do list.

Then there's the meeting at 9 AM that conflicts with the call at 9:30. Someone needs you in two places at once—again. Your phone buzzes with another text, another request, another demand on time you don't have. You haven't even left the house yet, and the weight is already crushing your chest.

By evening, you're physically home but mentally still at work. Your spouse is talking, your kids want attention, but you're nodding without hearing because your brain won't stop spinning. The guilt of being present but absent adds another brick to the load you're carrying.

The anxious heart weighs a man down.

Solomon writes of the weight of an anxious heart. Neuroscience aligns with the old king's proverbs. Cortisol, a stress hormone, creates toxicity in the brain that truly slows, if not cripples, our ability to think strategically or creatively. That toxicity affects all areas of our body, creating a 'weight.' You can see it in physical posture and countenance, like a person carrying a burden they can barely hold. We foresee possible dangers of loss that never come to be. Yet the possibility—the looming deadlines, the fear of failure, the threat of disappointing everyone—carries such weight even though most of what we dread never actually happens.

We live under constant threat. Not physical danger, but the psychological weight of never being enough, never doing enough, never having enough time. You can see the anxious heart in people's faces, their slumped shoulders, their exhausted eyes.

Power of a Kind Work

For those carrying this burden, there is nothing so timely and refreshing as a 'kind word' that 'cheers him up.' Think about a time when a friend cheered you up. Strength surges through your veins with a kind and encouraging word. **For a joyful heart is good medicine, but a broken spirit dries up the bones** (Proverbs 17:22).

If you are one today carrying a burden of anxiety, consider the cause or focus of your weight. Does your pain come from actual reality, or are you drowning in threat? Ask God for wisdom to see the difference. Write out your pain—describe the word or phrase that names it. Then 'cast your cares on the Lord for he cares for you' (1 Peter 5:7).

Entrust your burden to the Lord.

For those who walk lightly today, look around for the hurting who carry the weight of impossible expectations. Consider a kind word or deed that will cheer them up. Could it be that today, God has called you to be the hands and feet of Jesus to Someone drowning? Could it be that you may be a conduit of God's grace in their time of need? Consider the 'comfort we have received from God' (2 Corinthians 2:4). Now, do so in Jesus' name to those in need today.

Father, the weight of anxiety is crushing—help me cast my cares on You. Give me wisdom to see the difference between a real crisis and an imagined threat. Calm my racing mind. Make me a source of cheer and encouragement to others carrying impossible burdens today.

Guarded Life

*He who guards his lips guards his life, but he who
speaks rashly will come to ruin.* —*Proverbs 13:3*

Since my son was a little guy, we would talk about our words. Together, we would often quote, "Be quick to listen, slow to speak and slow to become angry" (James 1:19). Then we discuss the situation of the day to learn and grow. Both my son and I are in training on this idea. A sage's advice has spoken to many young people: **God has given you two ears and only one mouth for a reason**. So we heed the good counsel of the word and this wisdom to 'guard' our 'lips,' for it's a continual challenge.

A wise man once shared with me, *"Your reputation will protect you."* That idea took some time for me to absorb its truth. Its wisdom complements another idea that I've come to embrace, given to me by a friend years ago: *"You are responsible for your character, not your reputation."* Said another way, you cannot control what people think about you, only what you do and say that would validate their opinion. Validation may be good or bad. Some of these ideas have significant implications for your motives and actions relating to people, both personally and professionally. Such as, how much time do you spend in your day, or lying in bed at night, worrying about pleasing people? Or do you spend more time thinking, *or worrying,* over your character and the wisdom of what to say than doing the right thing? It's a challenge for all. Let us commit to grow in this way.

The idea of *guard* grips me. We see it written all over scripture. Here in Proverbs, we learn, "righteousness guards the man of integrity" (13:6) and "guard your heart for it is the wellspring of life" (4:23). *What's the cost of compromise of an unguarded life?* It comes at a significant cost.

That cost may be "ruin". We can all think of situations, maybe recent, where you've said something that you regret, for you know it came from an unguarded tongue that reflects an unguarded heart. Every time a careless word slips, it hurts. It hurts relationships by tearing them down instead of building them up. We all know the pain of this pattern.

Some incidents are purely situational—being in the wrong place at the wrong time, or encountering people who provoke reactions before you're ready to respond constructively. This is why we must embrace the discipline that **guarded lips create a guarded life.**

As my wise friend once told me: **"Your reputation will protect you."** Your reputation precedes you, which means that as your character matures, it naturally shields you from compromising situations and harmful influences. A strong reputation acts as a protective barrier, keeping you away from people and circumstances that could leave you vulnerable.

However, your reputation can serve as a type of 'guard' to protect you through respect, appreciation, or even curiosity. For the rash fool has a quick tongue, and its ruin is evident. Let us be wiser with a guarded tongue, thus guarding our life.

Father, guard my lips and my heart today, for they shape the character and reputation that either protect or expose me. Give me the discipline to be quick to listen and slow to speak, building up instead of tearing down with every word.

Fulfilled Satisfaction

*The sluggard craves and gets nothing, but the desires
of the diligent are satiated.* —*Proverbs 13:4*

C an you remember a time when you were stretched beyond what
you thought you were able to handle? When you had a task,
project, or goal that seemed nearly unachievable, yet by some miracle,
the impossible became possible. Do you remember that feeling? Do you
remember that moment of victory and accomplishment? Yeah, I do,
too... I also know the feeling of an expectation not being fulfilled. The
Lord leads us when we trust Him (Pr 3:5-6); He determines our steps
(Pr 16:9) when we make our plans, even if we're heading the wrong way.
Course corrections are not fun and often disappointing, even embar-
rassing, especially when we miss the mark due to a lack of diligence or
impatience and fail to wait on Him to provide direction.

Solomon captures a universal human experience: **"Hope deferred
makes the heart sick"** (Proverbs 13:12). We've all felt that heartache,
haven't we? Perhaps you're experiencing it right now.

If so, let me encourage you: **God's grace is sufficient.** His healing
grace can mend your broken heart. When your hope rests in the Lord
rather than your circumstances, everything changes. Solomon completes
the thought: when longing is fulfilled, it becomes **"a tree of life"**
(Proverbs 13:12).

If you're heartsick today, take a moment to remember when God fulfilled a deep longing in your life. Recall that moment when He brought
satisfaction and joy. Thank Him for it. Praise Him with an offering of

gratitude, because **"a longing fulfilled is sweet to the soul"** (Proverbs 13:19).

Your past fulfilled longings are proof of His faithfulness and a foretaste of what's yet to come.

Rekindle the sweetness of your soul and tap into the fulfillment found in the Tree of Life for what God has already done. *Beware of the sickness that comes from the ingratitude of what you don't have today by forgetting what God has already given.*

For 'the sluggard craves and gets nothing.' There is no fulfillment found from laziness and ingratitude that can feel like nothingness. *Get up!* Let your 'desires' and 'longing' be known to the Lord, commit your way to Him (Pr 16:3), 'delight yourself in the Lord and he will give you the desires of your heart' (Psalm 37:4). Now with a grateful heart... *Get moving!*... for 'the desires of the diligent are fully satisfied' (Pr 13:4). The Lord knows your dreams, desires, and ambitions completely. He will walk with you on the path. For together, with Him, no matter what you face today, you will be fulfilled and satisfied.

Father, I lay my heartache before you again today; you know the lack, yet I thank you for all that you have given. I give you thanks! Thank you for life, salvation, and your love in my heart. It is enough! You are enough! Give me the strength to walk with diligence in the task before me today.

Milestone 5: Moving to Colorado

J une 8th, 2002, was a defining moment in my life that I remember as a point of true desperation. The story begins with exhaustion—being spread so thin in so many ways that I was failing at nearly everything. The roles I was carrying, the expectations I'd placed on myself, and the commitments I'd made to others had created a treadmill I didn't know how to escape.

When I went out to the back lawn of my Georgia farmhouse that fateful night, I cried out to God in absolute exhaustion. "I'm so tired. I'm so tired. I'm so tired." I repeated those words as a desperate cry to the Lord. I needed His help, guidance, and direction because I didn't know how to escape this relentless treadmill of life.

Something during that evening resonated in my spirit in a way that perhaps not in an audible voice but with unmistakable clarity—I truly sensed I heard from the Lord that night: "Move. I'm calling you to move to Colorado."

Sobered by such a thought that resonated in my soul and spirit, I found myself in this strange tension of wondering if it was too good to be true. Did I hear that correctly? What would that even look like? Yet, I was simultaneously excited about the possibilities that such a move might hold.

When I went back into the house after my moment outside, Cari must have seen the countenance on my face because she asked how I was doing. I looked at her and said, "I think we're supposed to move to Colorado."

She looked back at me and said, "I know." The Lord had similarly prepared her heart.

The context makes this even more remarkable. Growing up in Georgia was all I knew—family, friends, community, church. At that time, I'd been at the same church for almost fifteen years. To move to the completely unknown, to be uprooted, and to step out on faith, spreading my wings by relocating my family with my two young girls, was the most significant faith move I had ever experienced.

Not knowing exactly where, put me in a posture of trust more than anything else. The fear of the unknown could have been the very thing that kept me from moving forward, but instead, the fear of the Lord and trusting that He would guide and direct our steps is what launched us to step out on faith.

Within three months, we had sold everything, packed our bags, and moved to Colorado, which has now been our home for more than twenty years. We moved to pursue a life of adventure and faith, raising our kids in a place where we could experience more of God's country. But more than all the geographical benefits, this represented pursuing a life of faith.

This creates an interesting tension when considering how faith and wisdom sometimes seem to be at odds with one another. Wisdom might demand a more conservative or prudent approach, whereas faith is the very thing that pleases God—and that can sound counterintuitive or even counter to wisdom. To sit in that tension requires a posture of trust.

Our move to Colorado was a milestone that expanded our mustard seed of faith as we learned to walk with prudence and wisdom moving forward. Some might look at it and say it was the craziest thing we ever did, but often, the craziest ideas of stepping out on faith are the very things that define our lives. Operating in both faith and wisdom—that's the tension we get to walk in the pursuit of wisdom.

When Hope is Deferred

*Hope deferred makes the heart sick, but a longing
fulfilled is a tree of life.* —Proverbs 13:12

I know the sickness of the soul that comes from prolonged waiting.
I've felt the weight of expectations unmet, the ache of anticipating
fulfillment that seems perpetually delayed. Solomon's words capture this
universal human experience—the heart-sickness that comes when hope
is deferred month after month, year after year.

This isn't the temporary disappointment of missing a green light
or waiting in a long line. This is the deeper soul-weariness that comes
from waiting for the job opportunity that doesn't materialize, the relationship that doesn't heal, the dream that remains unfulfilled, or the
breakthrough that never comes. It's the kind of waiting that makes you
question whether God has forgotten you or if your prayers are bouncing
off the ceiling.

The Hebrew word for "sick" here suggests more than physical ill-
ness—it's a languishing of the spirit, a withering of hope itself. When
our deepest longings remain unmet, something vital within us begins to
fade. We may continue going through the motions, but the joy leaks out
of daily life.

Dreams that once energized us now feel like cruel reminders of what
we lack.

Yet Solomon doesn't leave us in this place of heart-sickness. He offers
hope: "A longing fulfilled is a tree of life." The image is powerful—not
just relief from pain, but flourishing, growth, and vitality restored. The

Tree of Life represents abundance, healing, and renewal that flows from seeing our deepest desires satisfied.

But how do we bridge the gap between deferred hope and fulfilled longing? The pursuit of wisdom promises answers through insight, understanding, and favor. This isn't passive waiting but active seeking—engaging with God and His truth while we wait.

We can find understanding through multiple channels. First, we can draw on the counsel of the Holy Spirit, who guides us into all truth and whispers comfort to our anxious hearts. Second, the Word of God provides perspective on our circumstances and reminds us of God's faithfulness throughout history. Third, from an honest evaluation of our experiences—reflecting on how God has worked in our past seasons of waiting and what He might be teaching us now.

Wisdom is available in private 24/7 from the Lord. It's an incredible resource available to believers if we simply seek it through prayer, Scripture, and quiet reflection. In these private moments with God, we often find the strength to continue and the perspective to endure.

However, when private wisdom finds the courage to become public among trusted friends, the gift of understanding takes on a whole new dimension. Sharing our struggles with safe people multiplies our wisdom exponentially. They offer perspectives we can't see, encouragement we desperately need, and prayers that strengthen our faith.

Too often, we suffer alone, thinking our struggles are unique or that vulnerability equals weakness. But isolation compounds heart-sickness, while the community provides healing. When we risk sharing our deferred hopes with trusted friends, we discover we're not alone in our waiting. Others have walked similar paths and can offer both empathy and insight.

Father, You know the longings of my heart and the weariness of prolonged waiting. Transform my heart-sickness into patient trust. Give me wisdom to understand Your timing and grace to wait well. You are the tree of life, and in You, all my longings find their ultimate fulfillment.

Poor Pretender

One person pretends to be rich, yet has nothing;
another pretends to be poor, yet has great wealth.
—Proverbs 13:7

The rumble of my Papa's 1969 baby blue GMC still echoes in my memory. That old truck, with its "3 on the tree" gear shift, cost him exactly one dollar from his employer, US Steel. It was already weathered when he bought it. Still, to me, it represented everything admirable about his character—grit, prudence, and that unshakeable "work with what you've got" mentality that defined his generation.

Papa was a craftsman and a steelman. Buildings still stand today as monuments to his skilled hands, structures that have weathered decades since the 1950s through the 1980s. Yet he drove that humble truck with pride, never feeling the need to project wealth he didn't need to display. Both my grandfathers drove old trucks, and I can still smell the worn leather and motor oil, still feel the joy of riding in those truck beds, wind whipping through my hair.

Today's roads tell a different story. It's not uncommon to see $100,000 pickup trucks gleaming in every parking lot—technological marvels with luxury features that would make my grandfathers shake their heads in wonder. But here's what struck me: the sticker price doesn't necessarily reflect the character, skillset, or actual wealth of the driver behind the wheel.

Thirty years ago, "The Millionaire Next Door" revealed a startling truth that many found counterintuitive—most actual millionaires lived lives of frugality and prudence. The fun fact from the research in the late 90s was simple: most millionaires drove old pickup trucks. They understood that true wealth isn't about the image you project but the substance you build.

Proverbs 13:7 cuts through our pretenses with precision: "One person pretends to be rich, yet has nothing; another pretends to be poor, yet has great wealth." How many drivers of those gleaming $100,000 trucks are actually drowning in debt, desperately trying to project an image of success while their bank accounts tell a different story? How many, like my Papa, drive modest vehicles while building real wealth through discipline and wisdom?

The caution in today's proverb forces us to examine who we're trying to impress and why. Are we living for the approval of strangers at traffic lights, or are we building something lasting? Papa's old truck wasn't about impressing anyone—it was about transportation, utility, and stewardship. It led him to work on projects that mattered, things that would last.

The path of frugality might not turn heads on the highway, but it leads away from the trap of debt that disguises itself as prosperity. When we pretend to be rich through borrowed money and financed lifestyles, we become prisoners to payments, slaves to an image that owns us rather than the other way around.

Better to be the driver on the road of frugality, building real wealth in the shadow of an old truck, than to be trapped in the debt of pretended prosperity. Like Papa's GMC, true wealth might not look impressive from the outside, but it runs reliably and gets you where you need to go—toward genuine financial freedom and the peace that comes with it.

Father, give me wisdom to build real wealth through frugality and stewardship instead of pretending to be rich through debt and image. Help me value substance over appearance, choosing the security of living within my means over the slavery of borrowed prosperity that impresses strangers but owns my soul.

Teaching of the Wise

—◆○◆—

The teaching of the wise is a fountain of life, turning a man from the snares of death. —*Proverbs 13:14*

S top for a moment and imagine yourself on a scorching summer afternoon. The heat bears down mercilessly, sweat beads on your forehead, and your mouth feels parched. In the distance, you hear something—a gentle sound like wind rustling through leaves. Curious, you move toward the sound, and as you round the corner, you discover its source: a fountain of crystal-clear water spraying high into the air, creating a cool mist that refreshes everyone nearby. The contrast is immediate and profound—from oppressive heat to life-giving relief.

This vivid image captures our spiritual reality perfectly. In our daily demands, we often experience a different kind of dryness—the parched feeling of indecision, the exhaustion that comes from lack of clear direction, or the weariness of difficult circumstances. Just as that fountain provides physical refreshment, the timely word of a wise teacher brings spiritual renewal to our souls.

The proverb contains two powerful action words: **teach and turn**. These words demand honest self-examination. What path are you walking today that leads away from life? Perhaps it's a relationship that has grown toxic, a business decision driven by greed rather than integrity, a commitment you've made for the wrong reasons, or simply the gradual drift away from the wisdom that occurs when we stop paying attention. Life has a way of pulling us off course through seemingly small compromises that accumulate over time.

What decision lies before you today where you sense a *turn* needs to be made? Often, our reluctance to change direction stems from having no clear plan, no sense of where we're headed, no trusted counsel to guide us, or, worst of all, no hope that things can improve. We remain stuck in patterns that slowly drain our spiritual vitality simply because we can't envision a better way forward.

There's an ancient saying that transcends religious boundaries: "When the student is ready, the teacher will appear." This principle operates regardless of your background or worldview. But it raises crucial questions: Who is your teacher? More specifically, who are the wise voices speaking into your life right now? And perhaps most importantly, how good of a student are you?

Consider Jesus' teaching ministry—He instructed people in three distinct venues: publicly to crowds, privately to His disciples, and personally in one-on-one encounters. Each setting offered different depths of revelation and relationship. Today, wisdom comes to us through similar channels: the public teaching we receive in churches, books, and conferences; the private instruction that happens in small groups and trusted friendships; and the personal moments when God speaks directly to our hearts through His Spirit and Word.

The wise teacher serves as a fountain of life because their words don't just inform—they transform.

Who represents that fountain of wisdom in your life today? Are you positioned to receive from them? And equally important, are you becoming that fountain for others who desperately need life-giving direction? The teaching of the wise doesn't just benefit the receiver—it flows through them to refresh countless others walking in the desert of confusion and spiritual dryness.

Father, lead me to fountains of wisdom who can refresh my parched soul and turn me from paths leading to death. Make me a fountain of life for others walking in spiritual dryness, speaking Your truth that transforms and redirects toward abundant life.

Favorable Wins

Good understanding wins favor, but the way of the unfaithful is hard. —Proverbs 13:15

E ach day presents new opportunities that can be stimulating, exciting, and truly satisfying when accomplished. The size and significance of these opportunities reveal something important about timing and perspective—the larger the objective, the longer it takes to achieve its completion. This reality requires both patience and understanding.

Every opportunity brings new challenges. Each one presents fresh questions to be asked, problems to be solved, and a discovery process to find answers. The more significant the opportunity, the more complicated the solutions become. This complexity can become overwhelming when we get stuck focusing on problems without clear pathways to resolution.

I've watched this pattern countless times—in myself and others. We start with enthusiasm for a new venture, relationship, or goal. The initial excitement carries us through the early stages, but when complications arise, and solutions aren't immediately apparent, weariness sets in. Some lose interest and focus, which yields discouragement about venturing into the next opportunity. We can truly lose heart when opportunities slip away or prove more difficult than anticipated.

Can you relate? Maybe you're there today—stuck between the excitement of possibility and the frustration of complexity. If so, there's hope, and it's found in Solomon's wisdom about understanding.

"Good understanding wins favor" suggests that developing a deeper comprehension of our situations, relationships, and challenges leads to more positive outcomes. When we invest time in truly understanding the complexities we face rather than being overwhelmed by them, we position ourselves for success. This understanding isn't just intellectual—it's practical wisdom that helps us navigate complex and challenging situations.

Understanding people's motivations helps us build stronger, more effective relationships. Understanding market dynamics enables us to make more informed business decisions. Understanding our own strengths and limitations allows us to make more informed commitments. This kind of understanding doesn't come quickly or easily—it requires patience, observation, and often costly experience.

The contrast is stark: "The way of the unfaithful is hard." The unfaithful here doesn't just refer to marital infidelity but to anyone who lacks steadfast commitment to wisdom, truth, and growth. When we're unfaithful to the process of gaining understanding—when we want quick fixes, shortcuts, or easy answers—life becomes unnecessarily complicated.

The unfaithful person jumps from one opportunity to another without learning from past experiences. They repeat the same mistakes because they haven't invested in understanding why things went wrong before. They struggle in relationships because they haven't developed an understanding of how people work. They face unnecessary hardships because they've been unfaithful to the patient work of gaining wisdom.

But good understanding changes everything. It wins favor with God, with people, and even with circumstances. When we understand timing, we don't rush premature opportunities or miss appropriate ones. When we know people, we build trust and cooperation. When we understand our own patterns, we can break destructive cycles and create positive ones.

The pathway forward requires faithfulness to the process of gaining understanding. This means staying curious when things get complicated rather than giving up. It means asking better questions instead of demanding easy answers. It means learning from both successes and failures rather than simply moving on to the next thing.

Father, grant me a good understanding that wins Your favor and opens doors of opportunity. Help me be faithful to the process of gaining wisdom rather than seeking shortcuts. When opportunities become complicated, give me the patience to understand rather than the impulse to abandon them. Make me someone who learns from experience and grows in wisdom through both success and failure.

Secure Fortress

Whoever fears the Lord has a secure fortress, and for their children, it will be a refuge. —*Proverbs 14:26*

The day begins with many unknowns, whatever way the winds blow. So many things before me today beyond my influence or control. A crisis of confidence looms in the unknown. The last thing I feel is a sense of security. Weariness and impatience tempts me to give way to my insecurities. I feel my vulnerability and weakness so closely. What should I do with my fear? Then, I'm reminded!

Stand fast! We have a promise in the Lord today that no matter the threat or loss. He holds the cornerstone of what we truly hold dear. We do not have to be blown around by our insecurities but rather stand firm in the security of His fortress. We must direct our fears and concerns away from what fuels our insecurities. We take courage in the Lord, who will be a secure fortress. He is a haven no matter the status of our home.

"Therefore everyone who hears these words of mine and puts them into practice is like a wise man who built his house on the rock' (Matthew 7:24).

Let us take a stand on the rock of the word. We must hear and then act on its promises. Those under our influence are watching. Consider your 'fiery trial' and your responses. Consider those under your care. What are you modeling for those people who are observing your words, attitudes, and actions? For your fear will reveal itself through your actions, either as insecurity or as one in a 'secure fortress.' Stand firm on the rock and shelter of the Lord God, who can calm the storm, heal disease, and provide for all our needs.

For fathers and mothers, do your children need a refuge? When crisis strikes, all children need a secure and safe place. Do they find refuge in your love? If you see insecurity in your children, model with your words and actions what it looks like to live in the 'secure fortress' of God's protection. As you do, your children will learn to do the same in their time of testing and trial.

Regardless of age, as sons and daughters, no matter your loss or pain today, seek refuge in your Father's love. He is waiting with open arms to embrace you. Let go of your temporal fears and run to the only safe place that will never be shaken.

Father, when fear and uncertainty rise within me, draw me back to the shelter of Your steadfast love. May my trust in You be a living example that leads others—especially my children—to find refuge in Your unshakable fortress.

Committed to Success

Commit to the Lord whatever you do, and your plans will succeed. —*Proverbs 16:3*

High-capacity and competent leaders possess an incredible ability to accomplish things. There's a perception that everything they touch turns to gold. Yet, *the greatest strength of a leader may be their greatest weakness. The greatest enemy of great is good.* What distractions of good threaten God's great for you? God's will may not always be able to be measured in potential or promotion. For what is God's will? Many well-meaning believers have been stalemated with indecision. Yet, mature Christ followers know that God's will is found in pursuit of it. *A ship at port is hard to get moving, but on the open sea, the turn of the rudder and sail checks its heading.* As leaders, we are not often bound by indecision - our temptation is to make a decision too quickly. We lack the patience to 'wait upon the Lord' (Psalm 27:4). We risk sacrificing God's best for what we perceive as good and miss out on the great he has planned for us.

Commitment comes at a cost. There is a sacrifice for your resolve. Also, tucked into this powerful proverb is the discipline of trust. To commit your way is to entrust your motivations, thoughts, and plans to the Lord. Opportunities surround leaders, some of which are very compelling. Reflect for a moment on the NKJV translation of this same proverb, *'commit your works to the Lord, and your thoughts will be established.'*

Consider your thoughts. What are you thinking? Look at the opportunities before you today: time with the family, meetings, a creative initiative, vacation plans, a mission trip, a new business venture, a job opportunity, or a promotion. *Write it out. Define the opportunity, the cost, the reward, make a plan, and clarify your following action.* Then, step back and pray through your thoughts. You may find that you have more than one option or at least more than you can commit to. Again, beware of the distraction of good for the sake of the great. Let the Lord give you wisdom, insight, and understanding as you trust in him.

Measure your commitments by ordering your thoughts. Consider another reflective exercise to test your thinking by reading through Philippians 4:8. Would you define your thoughts and plans as 'excellent and praiseworthy'? We are called by God to a life of excellence even with all of its frailties. For his grace covers our weakness and makes us strong (2 Corinthians 12:9). Beware of feelings that would rob you of 'excellent and praiseworthy' thoughts and plans. 'Take every thought captive and make it obedient to Christ' (2 Corinthians 10:5b). As we submit our thoughts to Christ, we will have clarity and resolve to wholeheartedly 'commit whatever you do.' Ask the Lord today to 'establish your thoughts,' and you will find success. For God has great plans beyond what we can imagine (Jeremiah 29:13). His 'greatest' awaits us as we spend time in His presence and carry the grace of God into every thought, conversation, and commitment of our day.

Father, align my heart and mind with Your perfect will, that every thought and plan would reflect Your wisdom and purpose. Guard me from the distractions of what is merely good, and lead me to the greatness found only in Your grace and glory.

Pleasing and Peace

*When a man's ways are pleasing to the Lord, he
makes even his enemies live at peace with him.*
—Proverbs 16:7

One of God's most extraordinary works: transforming hostile relationships through our obedience. When we align our lives with God's ways, He doesn't just bless us—He changes how others respond to us, even those who once opposed us. The Lord provides guidance, precepts, and promises to direct us in His ways. When we fix our attention on Him, we naturally stay on the right path. Our focus truly determines our reality and direction. Think about a time when you lost your way spiritually. Where was your focus during that season? Most likely on yourself—your circumstances, your goals, your problems. Self-focus inevitably leads to spiritual drift. Today, deliberately turn your gaze back to the Lord. Allow your mind to be renewed by His truth, your heart restored by His love, and your focus recalibrated to pursue what pleases Him. This isn't merely positive thinking; it's the foundation for experiencing God's supernatural favor.

Never underestimate God's favor. God's favor extends far beyond our personal blessing. He possesses the power to turn the hearts and minds of those closest to us—and, remarkably, even our enemies. This isn't manipulation or coercion; it's the mysterious work of a sovereign God who responds to our obedience by softening hard hearts around us.

Reflect on the price of peace. What price are you willing to pay for genuine peace? Many people pursue peace through compromise, avoiding difficult conversations, or simply giving in to maintain harmony. But lasting peace requires a different currency.

In Christ, we discover the Prince of Peace. Yet claiming Jesus as Lord doesn't automatically grant us easy relationships. Sometimes, he becomes a stumbling block to others. As His disciples, we're called to follow him regardless of the cost, understanding that periods of conflict or even persecution may come.

Consider the miracle of Peace: when we consistently walk in God's ways, He can produce peace even with our enemies. This supernatural peace operates on multiple levels:

- **Inner peace** within our souls, regardless of external circumstances

- **Relational peace** with those we love and who love us in return

- **Miraculous peace**, even with those who oppose us

This peace far outweighs the pain of walking wayward paths. The alternative—a life focused on self, leading to brokenness and hurt—offers no lasting resolution. However, the path of pleasing the Lord leads to peace that not only transforms us but also everyone around us.

Father, guide me on Your path today. Give me wisdom to discern Your ways and strength to walk in them regardless of trials. Settle my spirit with Your peace. Grant me favor even with those who oppose me, that I may carry Your peace into every encounter. Let me speak words of peace to all I meet today.

Sweetness to the Soul

Gracious words are a honeycomb, sweet to the soul and healing to the bones.—Proverbs 16:24

T he meal looks perfect. Smells amazing. The presentation is flawless. Then you taste it and—disappointment. All appearance, without the flavor you hoped it had.

That's how my words land sometimes. All truth, no grace. Technically correct but impossible to swallow. Like a clanging cymbal pretending to be music.

I'm guilty of this. In coaching sessions, mentoring conversations, even at home with the people I love most—I see what's wrong, I know how to fix it, and I deliver the truth with all the gentleness of a hammer. Sharp. Direct. Efficient. And completely missing the sweetness that would make the medicine go down.

Paul warned about this: "If I speak with the tongues of men and angels, but have not love, I am only a resounding gong or a clanging cymbal" (1 Corinthians 13:1). I can speak perfect truth, have all wisdom, see precisely what needs to change—but if I don't deliver it graciously, I'm just noise.

Here's what I'm slowly learning: **truth without grace is my need to drive my agenda without empathy or compassion.** You can be entirely right and completely wrong at the same time. Right about the content, wrong about the delivery.

Think about the last time someone spoke gracious words to you in a difficult moment. Not fake positivity or sugar-coating hard truth—but genuine grace woven through necessary correction. It changed everything. The same message that could have crushed you instead strengthened you because of how it was delivered.

That's the honeycomb. A little sweetness makes what's hard to swallow good for your bones.

So why is this so difficult? Why do I default to sharp when I know gracious works better? Maybe it's impatience. Maybe it's pride—thinking my efficiency matters more than their dignity. Maybe it's fear that adding grace will dilute the truth.

But here's reality: **gracious words don't weaken truth; they strengthen it.** The sweetness isn't a compromise—it's wisdom. It's recognizing that people need both truth and kindness, correction and encouragement, honesty and hope.

Today, you'll have a challenging conversation. Someone needs to hear something difficult. You'll be tempted to say it straight—get it over with, rip off the bandage, tell it like it is.

Before you do, ask yourself: What would a little honey do here? Not to hide the truth, but to help it go down. How can you deliver what needs to be said in a way that strengthens rather than crushes?

Because here's the promise: when you add sweetness through gracious words, you don't just bless the other person. You heal your own soul, too.

Father, forgive my sharp tongue and impatient spirit. Teach me to speak truth wrapped in grace. Help me add sweetness to hard conversations today. Let my words be honeycomb—both true and kind, both honest and healing. Make me gracious like You.

Test the Heart

*The crucible for silver and the furnace for gold, but
the Lord tests the heart.* —Proverbs 17:3

S itting with some business leaders this week, we had conversations
about philanthropy. Those who have the means to give more, what
will they do when they get more? One observation was shared that
those who make more on their first business venture are often the most
cautious, careful, or tend towards hoarding. Yet, those who have made
it, lost it all, and then made it again are the most generous. The question
of how much is enough is typically answered with a response similar to
Rockefeller, 'just a little bit more.' *Resources such as money, power, and
position will not define your character. Instead, resources reveal or amplify
it.*

The crucible serves a purpose not to crush or destroy us but rather to
purify and refine our character. For 'you know the testing of your faith
develops perseverance. Perseverance must finish its work so that you may
be mature and complete, not lacking anything' (James 1:3-4). It's not an
easy message or method, but it's effective. Think of raising children; every
time we give a task, such as cleaning your room, studying for school, or
playing nicely with your brother, it is a form of a test. Time, training,
and discipline shape them, whereby the test becomes a joy rather than a
burden, with shoulders slumped for the task at hand; then, when they
celebrate their little victory of passing the test, we all celebrate together.

Think about your test; it could be a season from years past or a specific
event in the last week. How did you do through it? It's certainly char-

acter-revealing. Look honestly at your stumbling not as condemnation (Romans 8:1). No, instead, look at your need for God's grace and mercy, your need for wisdom that he gives generously, and a community to encourage and build you up. For your disappointment leads you to hope that doesn't disappoint (Romans 5:5). As you set your hope on the Lord through your test, you find your character has been developed. You are different than before. When you've rested after the weariness, you will find your mind renewed (Romans 12:1-2). You have been transformed and ready to do his will in humility, sober judgment, and the measure of faith God has given you through the test. For his grace is sufficient. (2 Corinthians 12:9). For let us say like the Apostle Paul, 'When I am weak, then I am strong' (10).

Most people, when asked about their trials, *say, 'I wouldn't want to go through that experience again, but I'm glad I did, for I'm better for it.'* How much more when we know that in our trials, the Lord tests and purifies our hearts. For we want to be clean, proper, and pure before the Lord and in his work.

The crucible and the furnace do reveal the heart. So, thank God today for the test, for you want to be God's conduit of grace to others. God wants to share his resources with you so they can be given through you. Let's not fall under the temptation for power, position, and money. Let us stand firm in the test so these may be instruments of blessing. In the test, we place our trust more in the giver than in the gifts.

Father, thank you for the test. Let my heart be clean before you today. Let me be an instrument of your will. I place my trust in you today above silver and gold.

I Got Your Back

Whoever would foster love covers over an offense, but whoever repeats the matter separates close friends. —Proverbs 17:9

O ur Friday men's group was discussing friendship—what it really means to have someone's back. We were sharing stories, getting philosophical about loyalty and trust. Then Matt, who was raised in New York with family connections to the Mafia, silenced the room.

"My dad used to say, 'You need a buddy to help you move. You need a friend to help you move a body.'"

Ten seconds of complete silence. Then we erupted in laughter—not because it was funny, but because of Matt's absolute sincerity and the shocking significance of what he'd just said. Talk about covering up an offense! That's loyalty taken to the extreme. But it raises the real question underneath the dark humor: **Who's got your back?**

Not "who will help you move furniture" but who will stand with you when everything falls apart? Who will extend grace to cover you when you mess up? Who protects you instead of exposing your weaknesses?

Love covers a multitude of sins. Not ignoring them, not pretending they didn't happen, but choosing not to broadcast them, rehash them, or weaponize them against someone you love.

Here's what I've learned about real friendship: everyone you love will hurt you eventually. Everyone. The question is what you do with that hurt. Some people collect offenses like evidence. They catalog every slight, remember every mistake, and keep mental files on every disappointment. And they bring them up. Repeatedly. "Remember when you said that thing three years ago?" "You always do this." "This is just like that time..."

Repeating the matter separates close friends. Every time you resurrect a buried offense, you signal that nothing is ever really settled. That no forgiveness sticks. That your friendship has an asterisk next to it with footnotes of everything they've done wrong.

This isn't about stuffing feelings. If something needs addressing, address it. Have the hard conversation. Clear the air. **But then cover it with God's grace and move on.** Don't keep talking about it—not to them, not to others, not even to yourself.

I've watched friendships survive massive betrayals because someone chose to cover the offense. Deal with it once, forgive it fully, then actually let it go. That's what "I got your back" really means—when you mess up, I'm not putting you on blast. I'm not keeping score. I'm covering it with love and moving forward.

Now, I'm not suggesting we take Matt's dad's advice literally about moving bodies. But the principle underneath? **Real friends cover for each other. They protect. They don't expose.** They foster love by letting things go instead of separating close friends by repeating offenses that should be buried.

Father, help me cover offenses with love instead of collecting them as ammunition. Give me friends who've got my back when I fail, and help me be that kind of friend to others—loyal, forgiving, and willing to let things go.

Friends And Brothers

A friend loves at all times, and a brother is born for a time of adversity. —Proverbs 17:17

When we were young, my brother and I roughhoused constantly. Wrestling on the living room floor, testing our strength. Running, climbing trees, and daring each other to go higher on the swing set. A competition that took place at home privately before we hit the schoolyard.

The rough and tumble of brotherhood, spurred on by adversity, fostered a form of friendship that also gave us both a little backbone. Especially as we grew. My brother filled out, and his punches got harder. **Healthy sparring. Healthy respect.** Don't tell him, but I think he's got more muscle than I do now, but I can still hold my own!

Friendship and brotherhood can go hand-in-hand. Yet **brotherhood stands over time, which always includes some adversity to overcome.** That's the difference —a friend loves at all times, but a brother is born for adversity.

Here's one thing I've learned in brotherhood that's served me well as a life lesson: **relationships bond through conflict.** The opposite can undoubtedly be true, bringing division instead of depth. But if you're able to stay with it—through the issue, the disagreement, the offense—it creates an even greater bond.

I'm grateful for the bond of brotherhood. Overcoming difficulties in life fortified our relationship through adversity. Those childhood wrestling matches prepared us for the real battles we'd face together as adults.

Yet **not all brothers are friends.** I can't choose my brother, but I can choose my friends. And I can choose to value, invest in, and love my closest friends well. A friend loves at all times—even when I'm not being a good friend. It's a choice to love others well.

Here's what's interesting to observe: the gift of your chosen friends who, over time, adversity, and commitment, become your brothers. **That's the real gift—brotherhood in friendship over a lifetime.** Friends who stick through the wrestling matches. Friends who stay in the ring when conflict comes instead of checking out when the heat is on.

In my years working with men, the greatest threat facing friendship and brotherhood today is isolation—being disconnected from one another. Men retreat instead of roughhousing. They avoid conflict instead of wrestling through it. They miss the sharpening that comes from relational proximity because they're unwilling to experience the friction.

But men who dare to stay connected—through adversity, through conflict, through hard conversations—discover something powerful. Their friendships become brotherhood. Their chosen friends become the brothers born for times of adversity.

Finally, note this: **it takes a long time to become old friends.** Wherever you are in the breadth and depth of friendship and brotherhood, keep making investments today for old friends tomorrow. Stay in the ring. Do the wrestling. Experience the heat. The bond that comes through staying is worth every uncomfortable moment.

Father, thank You for brothers—by-blood and by choice—who've stayed through adversity with me. Give me the courage to stay in relationships when conflict comes, knowing bonds deepen through wrestling instead of retreating. Help me invest today in friendships that will become brotherhood tomorrow.

Culture of Contagious Joy

A joyful heart is good medicine, but a broken spirit dries up the bones. —*Proverbs 17:22*

Hiking in the Colorado high country lifted my spirits on a perfect spring day. Blue skies stretched endlessly above, and fresh green growth was breaking through the winter's brown landscape, speaking of new seasons and fresh beginnings. The highlight of the hike wasn't the stunning vistas or challenging ascent—it was spending time with a dear friend whose presence always brightens any day.

As a young man, his nickname was "Tigger"—and he still carries that same irrepressible bounce in his step. His joy is genuinely contagious, lighting up every room he enters and energizing everyone around him.

So when we started up the trail, and I noticed his usual spark was dimmed, I knew something was seriously wrong. After some gentle probing, he shared the weight he'd been carrying: "This has been the hardest six months of my life, other than when my wife had cancer." This man knows real pain and heartache. He's lived under the threat of losing his sweetheart, faced financial pressures, and weathered storms that would crush many people's spirits.

Yet here's what struck me: even amid his broken season, surrounded by incredible mountain beauty and sharing honest conversation, I could sense both his current struggle and his underlying character. I don't know anyone who represents a sharper contrast between momentary brokenness and fundamental joy. His character remains one of contagious joy, even when circumstances threaten to dry up his bones.

This raises a crucial question for all of us: Do you carry contagious joy today, or are you bearing the weight of a broken spirit? More importantly, how do we cultivate hearts and minds of contagious joy, especially when life feels overwhelming?

- First, joy serves as a powerful antidote to anxiety. When threats and worries create a sense of danger that isn't always based on reality, God provides a pathway to guard our hearts and minds through prayer, petition, and thanksgiving. The preventive measure for anxiety isn't more planning or control—it's joy. "Rejoice in the Lord always. Again, I will say, rejoice!"

- Second, joy is fundamentally an attitude, not a circumstance. "Rejoice always, pray continually, give thanks in all circumstances"(1 Thes 5:16-18)—this trilogy isn't dependent on everything going well. It's a chosen posture of the heart that acknowledges God's sovereignty regardless of our situation.

- Third, joy assumes adversity will come. "Consider it pure joy when you face trials of many kinds" (James 1:2) isn't naive optimism—it's battle-tested wisdom. Rather than being taken out by difficulties, we take every thought captive, put on spiritual armor, take our stand, and choose to consider it joy.

My friend's temporary broken spirit doesn't negate his joyful character—it reveals the humanity we all share. Even the most joy-filled people face seasons when their bones feel dry, and their spirits feel crushed. But contagious joy isn't about never experiencing pain; it's about choosing hope, gratitude, and trust even when everything within us wants to despair.

Father, thank You for the medicine of a joyful heart. When my spirit feels broken, and my bones feel dry, remind me that joy is a choice, not a feeling. Help me cultivate contagious joy that serves as an antidote to anxiety, an attitude of gratitude, and an anchor during adversity.

Milestone 6: Career Crossroads

T he fall of 2010 found me in the back of my warehouse, experiencing what I can only describe as my "oh God moment." I was crying out to God once again, just as I had done nearly eight years before when we moved from Georgia to Colorado. But this oh God moment was different—it was more than burnout, more than exhaustion. It was truly a milestone moment that you might even call my genuine midlife crisis.

Being in my late thirties, I was experiencing what I would define as a holy discontent. There was a desperate cry coming from so deep within me, a desperate sense of belonging that felt like drowning. The question haunting me was simple yet profound: "Am I made for more than what I'm doing?"

I was running projects and operating a business that, at that point in my life, was completely running me. After surviving the economic downturn and facing a financial crisis, the entire business model underwent a significant shift, requiring me to pivot in ways I never anticipated. I found myself running from project to project, putting out fires every single day, with no end in sight.

Standing in that warehouse, I was crying out to the Lord, desperate for something fresh from Him to lead and guide my steps. I felt trapped in a cycle of survival rather than living with purpose and calling.

What emerged from that season was a fifteen-month journey of intense soul-searching. After that midlife crisis and desperate moment, I began pursuing mentors, coaches, and trusted friends who could help me navigate this crossroads. As I came out of that season, my milestone career moment required something that demanded more faith than perhaps I even had the courage to muster.

I had to step away from the security of fifteen years of running a business—the financial predictability that came with it, especially in a season of life with three kids, a house, a mortgage, and enormous responsibility. To step out on faith once again and start over in a career seemed both necessary and terrifying.

Looking back now, it's so significant that this was another one of those seasons requiring tremendous trust. On the surface, it didn't look very smart, almost foolish, to step away from the security, safety, and predictability of an established career. Yet something within me was calling, longing to move forward into uncharted territory.

During that transformative season, I gained deep awareness of how mentors, coaches, and friends had truly helped me develop and grow—and frankly, kept me from completely blowing up as a business leader. I emerged with a burning desire to provide the same support for other business leaders facing similar crossroads and crises.

If I could offer comfort, counsel, or courage simply by walking alongside them as a thought partner, that felt like something worth pursuing—not just as a ministry or hobby, but vocationally. I didn't even know where to begin, but that longing wouldn't leave me alone.

Here I am, all these years later, and that warehouse moment launched what has become my vocational calling. I've now been privileged to partner with hundreds of leaders across the globe—truly a miracle that began with a step of faith during a crisis moment when I wasn't even sure where to move forward. That's the pursuit of wisdom: trusting the Lord to direct your steps, even in the darkest moments.

Wisdom Words

The words of a man's mouth are deep waters, but the fountain of wisdom is a bubbling brook. —Proverbs
18:4

H iking in the Colorado high country in the springtime is awesome!
The leaves are coming out, and the brown mountainside landscape transforms into a life-giving green. When the sun is on your back
and you've finished your ascent to an amazing vista, there's nothing quite
like the descent into a valley or draw that flows with the cold winter snow
runoff. Moving from the hot trail on the ridgeline to the green shade near
a stream is so refreshing. When you're in the open country, you can hear
the water before your eyes see it, and your pace quickens. When you're
hot from the hill, there's nothing quite like the refreshment of your head
under a waterfall or your bare feet in a clear stream.

Do you have a season or journey that's left you a little overheated
with anxiety or exhausted from your pace? Whom do you turn to for
refreshing waters of wisdom?

Leaders are motivated by goals, solving problems, or new opportunities. We see a compelling vision and mission, then step into it. Yet, all
leaders face the reality that *growth creates challenges*. You may be stirred
with enthusiasm for a new work that is fresh and exciting.

However, most of us are simply staying steady under the vision we
are called to steward. Sometimes, the pressure feels overwhelming. You
can be at the end of your resources and ready to give up. Let me encourage you today. *Wisdom awaits you!* If you are exhausted and weary

from your run, let me give you a little perspective; it's normal and to be expected. There's an oasis of wisdom like water for your soul only a word away. Yet, you have to make the hardest choice of the day. Will you stop for a moment to be refreshed in wisdom? Will you take the time to acknowledge your fatigue and lack of wisdom? If you do, then you find God will refresh you, restore you, and grant you the resource of wisdom if you believe (James 1:5-6).

Step off the trail for a moment and refresh yourself in the waters of wisdom. Let the word of God and his promises bless you today (Psalm 1)(James 1:22-25). Then, consider who you should be walking with today. Who is a man or woman of wisdom in your circles that you can invite to rest, walk, or run with you today?

As a complement to today's verse on wisdom words, 'the purpose of man's are deep waters, but a man of understanding draws them out' (20:5). Who draws out the deep waters of you? Who do you draw out? There is a reservoir of wisdom waiting in a trusted community. It is found in a covenant community with God, who loves you, and a few trusted friends who will walk with you. Find your riverside today, refresh yourself and others, for wisdom awaits those who do.

Father, when my soul grows weary and my thoughts run dry, lead me to the refreshing streams of Your wisdom. Let Your Word and the counsel of godly friends renew my strength and fill me with life-giving insight for the path ahead.

Honor in Humility

———◆◇◆———

Before a downfall the heart is haughty, but humility comes before honor.—Proverbs 18:12

S itting in a leadership training with construction industry leaders, I watched a man at a crossroads. Twenty years in the trade. Skilled craftsman. Hard worker. But based on what he wrote during the assessment exercise, **his pride was getting in the way of building trust with his people.**

His command-and-control dictatorial style, which led from a confidence that smacked of arrogance, was keeping him from being approachable. He wasn't empowering his team—he was hoarding power. Creating compliance, not culture. Desperate to be respected at work and home, his pride had bullied his way to the next level of leadership. Now it was holding him back from going any further.

I've seen this pattern dozens of times. **Pride gets you to a certain level. Then it becomes the ceiling that keeps you from breaking through.**

Paul warns about this in Romans 12:3: "Do not think of yourself more highly than you ought, but rather think of yourself with sober judgment." That's what any leader needs—sober judgment about their leadership style. The ability to see clearly, not through the distorted lens of pride.

What he couldn't see was that his "my way or the highway" mindset was driving away the very people who could help him succeed. Three simple phrases felt impossible: "I was wrong." "I need help." "I don't have all the answers."

If he doesn't change, his career and relationships are in jeopardy. Not because he lacks skill, but because pride closes doors that only humility can open.

The warning is stark: "Before a downfall, the heart is haughty." Pride precedes the crash. **Pride is a heart issue**, and the biblical warnings about it weave throughout Scripture like a flashing red light we ignore at our peril.

James puts it bluntly: "God opposes the proud but shows favor to the humble" (James 4:6). **Our access to grace comes through humility.** When pride rules your heart, you're working against God's favor, not with it. At work and home, pride creates adversaries where humility creates allies.

Peter echoes the same truth: "Humble yourselves under God's mighty hand, that he may lift you up in due time" (1 Peter 5:6). If this construction leader desires honor—real respect, genuine influence, lasting leadership—the pathway begins with humility.

What does humility look like? Letting his guard down. Inviting different ways of doing things. Admitting when he's wrong. Asking for help when stuck. Empowering his team instead of controlling them.

Humility isn't weakness. It's strength is under control. It's secure enough in who you are that you don't need to prove it constantly. And here's the beautiful promise: **humility opens the way to relationship.** With God. With your team. With your family. The blessing of grace, trust, and honor comes wrapped in humility.

Father, I confess my pride, forgive me for any discrimination from my need to get my own way—help me think of myself with sober judgment instead of more highly than I ought. I will look to you to lift me up. Thank you for your grace in humility.

Generous Giver

A gift opens the way for the giver and ushers him into the presence of the great. —*Proverbs 18:16*

T hree simple questions emerge from Solomon's profound observation about the power of generous giving: What's your gift? Who are the givers? Who are the great?

What's Your Gift?

The Hebrew word for "gift" here encompasses more than material presents—it includes talents, resources, time, attention, and acts of service. Your gift might be financial generosity, but it could equally be the gift of encouragement, hospitality, or skilled craftsmanship. Perhaps you can listen deeply, solve problems creatively, or bring joy to even the most challenging situations.

Some people possess the gift of opening doors for others through introductions and connections. Others give the gift of wisdom through mentoring or the gift of comfort during times of loss. The mother who gives her children the gift of patient instruction, the neighbor who gives the gift of practical help, the friend who gives the gift of loyal presence—all are generous givers whose gifts open ways and create access.

The key insight is that everyone has gifts to give. The question isn't whether you have something valuable to offer but whether you're willing to give it generously. Hoarded gifts benefit no one, but shared gifts create pathways that didn't even exist before.

Who Are the Givers?

Generous givers aren't necessarily the wealthiest people in terms of money, but they're always the richest in Spirit. They understand that giving isn't about having excess to spare—it's about having a heart willing to share. The widow who gave her last two coins demonstrated this principle perfectly.

True givers recognize that everything they possess ultimately belongs to God. They see themselves as stewards rather than owners, managers rather than hoarders. This perspective liberates them to give freely because they trust that God will provide for their needs as they meet the needs of others.

Generous givers also understand timing. They know when to offer practical help, when to provide emotional support, and when to offer financial assistance. They're sensitive to the Spirit's prompting and to the genuine needs around them.

Who Are the Great?

The "great" in this proverb aren't necessarily famous or powerful, though it can include them. The truly great are those who possess influence, wisdom, and the ability to positively impact lives. They might be business leaders, community influencers, spiritual mentors, or simply people who have walked difficult paths and gained valuable insights.

Interestingly, generous giving opens doors to these people not through manipulation or quid pro quo arrangements but through the natural attraction that generosity creates. Great people are drawn to generous hearts because they recognize kindred spirits—others who understand that true greatness comes through giving rather than getting.

The ultimate "great" presence we're ushered into through generous giving is God Himself. When we give as He gives—freely, lovingly, sacrificially—we align ourselves with His heart and character. Our generosity becomes a form of worship that opens the way to deeper intimacy with Him.

Father, help me discover and develop the gifts You've placed within me. Make me a generous giver who shares freely rather than hoards selfishly. Open my eyes to see the needs around me and my heart to respond with Your love. Use my generosity to open doors of relationship and influence that honor You and bless others.

Unoffendable

---◆◇◆---

*A man's wisdom gives him patience; it is to his glory
to overlook an offense. —Proverbs 19:11*

N ot long ago, an older woman visited my wife. Her hands and feet
are crippled with rheumatoid arthritis, and she's clinically blind
enough that she no longer can drive. Just being with her causes you
to slow your pace to listen more clearly to the wisdom of this patient
lady. She shared with my wife a desire to live in a posture of being
unoffendable. Wow! What a vision for all our lives. Yet, it comes with
time, wisdom, and exercised patience.

When you have high expectations of people or their performance, it
becomes a vulnerable place. It is easy to be disappointed, and that quickly
leads to frustration, bitterness, anger, and unforgiveness. We've all been
there with people in our lives. If we're honest, we're there with ourselves.
Who do you need to forgive? How do you need to heal from a past hurt?
It's been said *that hurt people hurt people*. When does the cycle of offensive
end? When will we arrive with enough wisdom and, thereby, patience to
be beyond offended?

Imagine living free from offense. Freedom! Unoffendable! Really, free
from carrying the baggage and bondage of hurt from a parent, spouse,
child, friend, pastor, colleague, or boss.

Take stock today of offensives in your heart. Take it to the Lord
and release that offensive and hurt today. As you walk in that freedom
today, ask the Lord for continued wisdom so as not to take on the same
offensive in the following incident. Let there be grace and wisdom on

your tongue for the hurt person who has hurt you. Let us be wise to the boundaries we need in our hearts for those who easily offend us until we are strengthened in our freedom of forgiveness. Let's be wisdom and grace givers today for all those in our lives regardless of the depth of history. Let us forgive to the measure we have been forgiven. Let us walk in that grace and glory today that we have overlooked an offense as our Lord has done with us.

Lord, thank you for your forgiveness. Strengthen me today to walk in the grace of being unoffendable. Grant me the grace to heal from past hurts. Please grant me wisdom and patience. Grant me a heart ready to forgive an offense and offer the same grace you have given me.

Father, fill my heart with Your wisdom and patience so that I may live free from offense and quick to forgive. Teach me to release the need to be right and to reflect Your grace toward those who have hurt me.

Lending Generously

———◆◦◆———

Whoever is kind to the poor lends to the Lord, and he will reward them for what they have done.—Proverbs 19:17

I was eight years old, sitting in the back seat of our old white Chrysler. Mom was going from church to church around the area, asking for help to cover utilities and rent. The divorce had left us in tough times financially, and I remember the weight of those moments—the shame of waiting in the car while she went inside, the uncertainty of whether we'd have electricity or a place to live.

Those memories shaped my heart toward generosity in ways I couldn't have understood then.

Years later, when God blessed us with means, those back-seat memories became the motivation for how we'd live. We supported families struggling to make ends meet. We created employment opportunities for people in my warehouse who needed work. We hired young mothers who could work from home while their little ones napped, making calls for my business and providing them with income without sacrificing time with their babies.

I couldn't erase the memory of my mom asking for help. But I could become the person who answered when someone else asked.

Paul writes in Philippians 4 about knowing "what it is to be in need, and I know what it is to have plenty. I have learned the secret of being content in any and every situation." That secret isn't just gratitude—it's wisdom about managing expectations. **Understanding the difference**

between what I need and what I want so I can help others in need is essential.

When you've sat in the back seat wondering if the lights will stay on, you develop a different perspective on "necessities." The $100,000 truck becomes absurd when you remember praying for $100 to keep the power on. The luxury vacation feels empty when you know families who can't afford groceries.

This is where Proverbs 19:17 becomes revolutionary: "Whoever is kind to the poor lends to the Lord." When we give to those in need, we're not just being charitable—we're literally lending to God. And He promises to reward what we've done.

That eight-year-old in the back seat received kindness from strangers who lent to the Lord. Now I get to be on the other side of that equation—creating opportunities, offering help, being generous not because I'm wealthy, but because I remember being poor.

It requires wisdom to be a blessing. To know when to give. How much to give? What kind of help actually helps? But when we lend to the poor, we're lending to the Lord Himself.

Father, thank You for the people who helped us when I was eight and we had nothing—they were lending to You. Give me wisdom to be generous with what You've entrusted to me, always remembering what it felt like to be on the receiving end of Your provision through others' kindness.

Plans, Purposes, and the Path

Many are the plans in a man's heart, but it is the Lord's purpose that prevails. —Proverbs 19:21

On a recent trip to Kansas City, I had breakfast with a pastor and dear friend. We discussed numerous ideas and possibilities, but one statement he made on that trip has stayed with me, representing a profound life lesson: "God will shape you by chipping away at your ideals in the context of the reality of your circumstances."

This insight struck deep. What are my ideals—those best intentions and plans that I hope will become reality? What current realities challenge those ideals? The convergence of both creates the tension where God does His shaping work. Our hopes, dreams, desires, and even fears govern the passions that motivate us to pursue our ideals.

I find great comfort in submitting to God's plans over my own, yet I must confess—I have many plans. They're wrapped up in my ideals, and my mind continually works through ideas that stimulate me to action. My plans range from building a home and pursuing seminary to raising a family and starting a business. Every day brings plans, from the most minor task details to lifelong work governed by God's call on my life.

Let me offer an illustration from our family game nights. My kids and I love playing Spades—a simple card game where each person plays a card, and the highest number takes the trick. But here's the key: whether or not an ace is played, a 2 of spades still trumps everything. That's the trump card that changes the entire game.

Are the Lord's purposes the trump card of our lives? Or do his purposes provide boundaries and room to move without going off course? Scripture is clear—when we submit our ways and plans to the Lord, he will direct, guide, counsel, and prosper our steps.

As a father, I give my children space to play, but when they approach danger, I step in to guide and protect them. When we're deciding something as simple as where to eat dinner or which movie to watch, everyone gets to weigh in, but ultimately, the decision rests with my wife or me. We have a broader perspective and final authority.

This raises a crucial question: How tightly do I hold to my plans when weighing them against the Lord's prevailing purposes? My ideas and plans need continual submission to the Lord. I must remain aware of what drives my heart, thoughts, words, and actions and then submit everything to him for his direction and purposes.

The beautiful tension is this: God doesn't discourage us from planning—He encourages wise planning. But he also reminds us that his purposes ultimately prevail.

Sometimes, God fulfills our plans exactly as we envision them. At other times, he chips away at our ideals through circumstances we never anticipated. Both experiences shape us into the people he's designed us to become. The key is holding our plans loosely while holding his character firmly.

When our plans align with his purposes, we experience the joy of partnership with God. When they don't, we learn the more profound joy of trusting his wisdom over our own understanding. Either way, his purposes prevail—not to frustrate us but to fulfill us in ways we couldn't have imagined.

Father, thank you for my ideals, but with your help and by your grace, I bring them into submission to your reality today. I pray like Jesus: not my will but Yours be done, not my kingdom but Your kingdom come, not my glory but Yours alone. Help me plan wisely while trusting completely in Your prevailing purposes.

Deep Waters

The purposes of a man's heart are deep waters, but a man of understanding draws them out. —Proverbs 20:5

I t has been said that men use approximately 15,000 words a day, compared to women, who may use around 50,000. The counts may vary by day and personality, yet the ratios and quantities are generally accurate. *Would you say that's true for you?* It has also been observed that women relate, while men report. Women tend to share their feelings more easily than men. Whereas when men share what they think and anchor their comments to the facts. What percentage of what men say every day has to do with business, sports, and weather? Maybe these subjects are safe, factually debatable, and easy to report. So, when do men express what they feel? Over the years, I've spent time with hundreds of men and noticed a trend among them. *Men feel deeply!*

Men have deep waters! Yet, you may not know it by first impressions or surface talk. Men are protectors by nature and, therefore, guarded. We keep the walls up and doors closed. We often have a tendency to hide behind our thoughts and feelings, which can leave us vulnerable. So, why do we respond this way? After volumes have been written, countless debates over decades, and thousands of hours of counseling, a straight-forward word surfaces from the deep waters of complexity represented within men's hearts. *TRUST. Whom do we trust?* For most men, the list is very short! For the men reading, I challenge you to take a moment and write down the names of men you trust. Don't worry, it won't take you very long. Your God-given instincts have already fired, and you have the answer. The list is short. Who do you trust? Write it down and let your mind and heart resonate with the answer.

Now, I would like to address a LIE that some men have accepted deep in their psyche. YOU ARE SHALLOW. Gentlemen, that is a lie; it's a lie; you have 'deep waters' running through you. Words that may have been spoken over you, such as artificial, superficial, or poser. There are likely other words that have spoken over you that keep you crippled in shame and fear, and keep you from drawing out your 'deep waters." Let's recognize the lie and embrace the truth that there is so much more to you than what you may have represented today. God has placed 'deep waters' inside of you for a reason. He wants to call you out today to live from those 'deep waters.' It's time to break the vow of distrust. Embrace God, who you can trust.

You can trust God with your life. As you do, he will bring 'men of understanding' around to draw out those 'deep waters.' *It's a risk with a great reward.* For courage, strength, wisdom, and faith await you. These are the 'waters' to refresh you and those people in your life. If your trust has been broken in the past, there's grace and mercy ready for the asking. God wants to refresh you in his ocean of deep waters. For that is the source of your deep well. Will you trust him? Will you trust a few' men of understanding' to draw out your 'deep waters'?

Father, thank You for placing deep waters within my heart—wells of purpose, courage, and truth. Help me trust You fully and allow others of understanding to draw out the depth You've placed in me for Your glory and the good of others.

Beware of the Silver Tongue

Food gained by fraud tastes sweet, but one ends up with a mouth full of gravel. —Proverbs 20:17

G rowing up in an entrepreneurial family, I learned early on about business, negotiation, and deal-making. In the early '80s, a book called "The Art of the Deal" captured the imagination of ambitious businesspeople everywhere. The concept was intoxicating—that you could master the art of persuasion, positioning, and strategic negotiation to consistently win.

I absorbed that mindset like a sponge. Watching my family navigate business deals, learning the language of leverage, understanding how to read people and situations. There was something exhilarating about it—the chess match, the strategic thinking, the satisfaction of closing a deal on favorable terms. Here's the problem...

The art of the deal can border on manipulation. And it tastes sweet—until it leaves a pit in your stomach.

Early in my career, as a young businessman, I was warned about the silver-tongued salesman. But nobody told me I might become one. Nobody warned me that "all life is sales" could become an excuse for using words as weapons instead of tools for genuine service. Getting someone to buy what you're selling, no matter how close to the line of truth, even socially acceptable manipulation—it starts sweet and ends with rocks in your gut. You got what you wanted, but you may have compromised who you are. You influenced someone through their weakness, their ignorance, their insecurity. You won, but it feels like losing.

There's a better way. There's a difference between *serving someone and selling* them, between helping them make a good decision and manipulating them into a bad one. Beware of the bread that tastes so sweet. Now I'm further along in life and I see silver tongues everywhere. Social media influencers. Politicians spinning stories. Preachers using emotional manipulation. Salespeople who care more about their commission than your actual needs. And I recognize the techniques because I used them.

So here's what I've learned: **Words are power, and power reveals character.** Are you using words to serve or to take? To illuminate or to confuse? To help someone make a wise decision or to pressure them into your agenda?

Actual sales—the noble kind—help people. It moves good products and services to those who need them. It creates value for everyone involved. But manipulation? That's just bread that turns to gravel.

Pay attention to the pit in your stomach. It's telling you something. And watch for the silver tongues around you—the people whose words sound great but leave you feeling confused, pressured, or manipulated.

Father, forgive me for the times I've tried getting my own way, selling rather than serving. Give me discernment to recognize silver tongues, including my own. Help me use words to illuminate truth, not obscure it. Let my yes be yes and my no be no. Keep gravel out of my mouth.

Dangers Of Cancel Culture

If anyone curses their father or mother, their lamp will be snuffed out in pitch darkness. —Proverbs 20:20

I 've watched it destroy families. One offense—sometimes from decades ago—becomes the reason to cut off all contact. Forever. No conversation. No reconciliation. Just complete separation, justified by the language of "boundaries" and "self-care."

Cancel culture isn't just wrecking public figures. It's wrecking families.

Let me be clear: I'm not talking about situations of genuine abuse or danger. Sometimes distance is wisdom. Sometimes boundaries are necessary for survival. But that's not what I'm seeing most often.

What I'm seeing is families separated for generations over things that could have been talked through. Parents cut off from grandchildren over political disagreements. Siblings are refusing to speak because of a slight from a wedding fifteen years ago. Adult children walking away completely because their parents weren't perfect.

Here's what nobody wants to hear: **there are no perfect parents.** None. Not yours. Not mine. Every single person who raised you made mistakes, said things they regret, and failed you in some way. The question isn't whether they were perfect. It's whether you're going to honor them anyway. The fifth commandment doesn't come with disclaimers: "Honor your father and mother... unless they disappointed you." It just says honor them. And it comes with a promise—that it may go well with you and you may enjoy a long life.

I've walked this road for decades. My parents weren't perfect. I could build a case for why I had every right to walk away. But I made a different choice: to honor them anyway. Not because they earned it every moment, but because **the alternative leads to darkness.**

That's what this proverb warns: curse your parents, and your lamp gets snuffed out—it's just how spiritual reality works. Unforgiveness, bitterness, and permanent separation don't just hurt the relationship. They put out your light. I've seen it. People who cut off their families and wonder why life feels so dark. Why relationships keep failing. Why they can't shake the shadow that follows them. They think they're protecting themselves. They're actually snuffing out their own lamp.

So what do we do with imperfect parents? We have the hard conversations. We extend grace we didn't receive. We give honor where honor is due—not for what they did perfectly, but for what they gave us at all. This isn't about pretending everything was fine. It's about breaking curse cycles. It's about choosing blessing over bitterness. It's about recognizing that walking in perpetual offense keeps you in darkness.

Here's the balance: Set healthy boundaries where wisdom requires it. Speak truth about real harm that was done. Get counseling if you need it. Take time to heal. But permanent separation over imperfection? That's different. That's choosing to snuff out your own lamp. Unless there's genuine danger or ongoing abuse that makes a relationship impossible, complete cancellation trades temporary relief for lasting darkness. The lamp that gets snuffed out isn't just a metaphor—it's the light in your own life, your own future, your own soul. Choose wisely what you're willing to lose in the name of self-protection.

Father, this is hard. Some of us carry real wounds from imperfect parents. Help us discern between wise boundaries and cursing separation. Give us grace to honor where we can, forgive where we must, and break cycles of bitterness. Don't let unforgiveness snuff out our lamp. Light our way toward reconciliation where possible and peace where it's not.

Splendor of Silver

The glory of young men is their strength, gray hair the splendor of the old. —Proverbs 20:29

E very month at the barbershop, the black drape tells the truth my mirror sometimes hides. As silver clippings fall around the chair, I'm reminded that my hair has been quietly transforming—what the barber generously calls my "platinum highlights" are simply the silver threads of time weaving through what remains of my natural color. Recently, I switched to a barbershop that uses gray drapes instead of black ones. The softer backdrop is kinder, but no amount of lighting or gentle draping can change the reality: the blond-haired boy I once was became a brown-haired young man, and that young man has become silver-haired today. One day, I may carry the same white crown as my Grandpop wore. The monthly haircut serves as an undeniable reminder—I'm getting older.

What's your strength? What's your splendor? For all of us, our glory is somewhere in between. It's a serious question. Life's challenges can cause us to stumble and fall, bringing hurt and hardship. Just this week, my friend's 13-year-old son suffered a knee injury from football training. His recovery will be many months, and I hope he recovers his confidence to step back out on the field. Also, this week, I sat with a 70-year-old white-haired businessman who had recently lost over a million dollars on a venture. He confessed his lack of courage and confidence to step back out on the field as a mentor to young men. He felt that he had nothing to offer. Oh my, that man has much strength and splendor in his wisdom.

Be encouraged! No matter your age or season, we all have challenges that would threaten to diminish our passions and purpose. The Apostle Paul says to us, 'Therefore we do not lose heart. Though outwardly we are wasting away, yet inwardly we are being renewed day by day (2 Corinthians 4:16). Despite the hardships you've faced on the exterior, let God restore and renew you on the inside. It's God's grace that gives strength when you are weak. It's God's glory that glorifies you to be a light in your areas of influence.

Young men love showing their strength. They are always looking for opportunities to test their manhood. Older men often enjoy sharing their wisdom, even though they may claim to have little of it. Age and experience do not always produce wisdom. Yet, in 'the man's heart are deep waters.' Men of splendor may need a man of understanding to draw them out. (Proverbs 20:5). Both young and old have strength and wisdom to offer one another. We are better to have both in our lives.

To the young man, do you have a gray-haired wise man in your life? To the older man, do you have a young buck that you may impart wisdom and benefit from his strength of vitality, curiosity, and ambition? For both, you may find that each acts as a catalyst for God's inward renewal. Take a moment today to think about the blond, brown, black, red, silver, and white-haired men in your life.

Think of ways to draw out their glory and splendor. Find ways to encourage and build up these men in strength and wisdom. For in doing so, you will be both strong and wise as you impart the same to another man.

Father, thank You for the strength of youth and the splendor of age, both reflections of Your grace at work in every season of life. Teach me to honor the wisdom of those who have gone before me and to use my strength to serve and encourage others for Your glory.

The King's Heart

---◆◇◆---

*The king's heart is a stream of water in the hand of the
Lord, He turns it wherever He will.—Proverbs 21:1*

When we think of kings today, we don't picture crowns and
thrones. We picture the people who hold power over our
lives—political leaders making policy decisions that affect millions. Business owners are determining the fate of their employees. Bosses are controlling our workdays. Professors shaping young minds. Teachers influencing the next generation. Pastors shepherding congregations. Parents raising children.

**All of them are "kings" in their spheres of influence, authority,
and power—for good or not.**

Here's what stops me in my tracks about this proverb: **the king's
heart is in the Lord's hand.** Not maybe. Not sometimes. Not only
if the king is righteous. The king's heart—whoever holds power—is a
stream of water that God channels wherever He pleases.

That changes everything about how we respond to authority. Our first
response shouldn't be anger, anxiety, or activism. **It should be prayer.**
Interceding on behalf of the kings and queens of our day, asking God to
direct their hearts like a river.

Think about it. That boss who seems immovable? That political leader whose decisions baffle you? That parent who won't listen?
That pastor who's stuck? **God can move them like water flowing
downhill.** He channels hearts. He redirects stubborn minds. He breaks
through resistance.

Sometimes it feels like those in authority are damned up—stuck in indecision when the people under their influence desperately need them to act. Employees need direction. Children need discipline. Congregations need leadership. Citizens need courage from their leaders. But the dam holds, and nothing flows.

God can break dams. He's done it before. He hardened Pharaoh's heart and softened it. He turned pagan kings into worshipers. He redirected entire empires through dreams and visions. If He can channel the heart of a king who doesn't even know Him, how much more can He move those who claim His name?

But here's where it gets personal: **if you have influence, power, and resources, this proverb is about you too.** Where does God need to move and direct your heart like a watercourse? What dam has formed in your life—stubbornness, fear, pride, comfort—that's blocking the flow God wants to channel through you?

If you need flow in your life—direction, breakthrough, movement—He can act on your behalf. But you have to let Him. You have to surrender control of the channel and let Him direct the stream.

Father, I intercede today for the kings in my life—those in authority over me and those under my rule. Channel their hearts like water toward Your purposes. Break through the dams of indecision, stubbornness, and fear. And Lord, direct my own heart—remove whatever's blocking Your flow through my life and channel me toward all who please You.

A Good Name

A good name is more desirable than great riches; to be esteemed is better than silver or gold. —Proverbs 22:1

Years ago, my friend Peter encouraged me to consider *you're responsible for your character, not your reputation.* That is a guiding principle that can keep us steady and on the narrow path. The character of 'humility and the fear of the Lord bring wealth and honor and life" (22:3). These are the things that we desire most, yet they come first from the character. Character is only tested in times of extreme, either in abundance or crisis.

My first real crisis in business occurred in 2000 when a client went bankrupt during the middle of a significant project. My response was to diligently recoup some of my losses, which were significant for my standards. We nearly went under as a business. I was scared. Fear is not an effective motivator to develop a healthy business. In addition, *desperate people often do desperate things;* in my case, I took a greater risk by trying to grow a business and its infrastructure too quickly, and I funded the business through debt and risky projects. As the volume increased, so did the volatility. Deals fell apart because I couldn't service my clients. After five years of good business in the marketplace, my reputation began to suffer due to my inability to deliver on my commitments. It cost me in more ways than just business.

It is a fine line of your focus between silver or gold versus a good name, honor, and life that comes from humility and the fear of the Lord. Most of us are bound by the bottom line of our pride or fear rather than the Lord. For the Lord has a different economy of scale.

Let us be mindful of our motivations and wise in our commitments, letting our 'yes' be 'yes' and our 'no' be 'no' (James 5:12). Then let us be wise about our character. What is in our heart? Pride and fear focus on people, power, and possessions of the world. Let us replace these by God's grace with the character of humility and fear of the Lord. Then, we will gain wisdom, insight, and understanding. As we focus more on these things, let us pray we will be esteemed with a good name.

How timely and instructive are the words written in the following verses; 'rich and poor have this in common; the Lord is the Maker of them all. A prudent man sees danger and takes refuge, and the simple keep going and suffer for it. (22:2,3). Let me live today as an image bearer of my Maker and my Lord. Let me be wise and prudent on the road ahead, pressing ahead with some opportunities and then seeking refuge where needed. I have been foolish and straightforward and have suffered for it. I pray no longer... Let me walk in the confidence of wisdom, humility, and the fear of the Lord.

Father, help me to guard my commitments, grant me the favor of a good name, and keep my heart in check to the lure of riches. Let me take on the character of Christ that I may reflect to all I meet today.

Father, shape my heart to value integrity over income and humility over honor, that my character may bring glory to Your name. Teach me to walk in wisdom and truth, trusting that a good name before You is the richest treasure I could ever gain.

Wealth, Honor, and Life

*Humility and the fear of the Lord bring wealth,
honor, and life. —Proverbs 22:4*

So few see the wisdom of humility. For who wants to be humbled? So few are willing to confront their fears. For truly, is there anything more terrifying? Rather, we carry pride and cover our fears under a shroud of wealth and respect. Yet, inside, we feel the emptiness and void, knowing the shallowness of pride and the terror of our fears. For this is not life but rather death.

Think of someone in your life who displays genuine humility. Is there anything more endearing and inviting than the authenticity of a humble heart? Now, think of someone who has faced their fears and found victory. Their fear has been replaced with a holy awe and fear of the Lord. Thus, their fears that once held them bound and crippled have been replaced with a measure of faith. Think of these people full of humility and faith. They are truly inspirational. Yet, their road has not been easy. Regardless of specific circumstances, we all face a daily choice: to humble ourselves before the Lord God or to cover ourselves in pride and self-sufficiency. We have the option to face our fears daily and lay them before the One who can take our fears and turn them into mighty courageous measures of faith.

For all desire wealth and honor. 'A good name is more desirable than great riches...' (22:1). We find these as we build trust and earn respect from those in our lives. People are drawn for a moment to the confidence that many carry in pride and accomplishment. Yet, if these are a pose or front to a broken soul, the honor you find in the moment may be short-lived. For the person drawn to these, it may have been self-seeking as well. What a miserable fellowship! For it is humility and faith found in a soul in pursuit and fear of the Lord that truly draws genuine respect and honor. These are the foundation for true friendship and fellowship.

Make the choice today to humble yourself before the Lord God. Lay down your pride and self-sufficiency. Seek the salvation of your soul in the Lord's grace. Speak out the darkness of your fears, confessing them before the Lord and bring light to your souls. For in confession and consecration, your worries will be turned to faith. For here, you will find a 'wealth' to your souls that may even yield itself materially in time. For here you will see 'honor' first from the Lord so he 'may lift you' (1 Peter 5:6). For here there is only death for your pride and fear, but this is the place where you will find 'life.' For God wants to bless you today with 'wealth, honor, and life.' Jesus spoke these words to his disciples and you today, ' I have come that they may have life and have it to the full' (John 10:10).

Father, teach me to walk in true humility and holy fear, laying down my pride and trusting fully in You. May Your wisdom fill me with the wealth of Your grace, the honor of Your presence, and the fullness of life found only in Christ.

Train Up A Child

---

*Train up the child in the way they should go, and
even when they are old, they will not turn from
it.—Proverbs 22:6*

There's a difference between discipline and training that every parent needs to understand. Discipline corrects wrong behavior. Training develops the right character. **Both are necessary, but they serve different purposes at different stages.**

My dad had a light hand. A look could stop me in my tracks. My mom, on the other hand, took a belt when necessary. And I'll never forget the time my friend's mom broke a wooden spoon on my backside because I desperately needed discipline—and I had none. She wasn't abusive; I was out of control, and someone had to step in.

That's discipline—corrective action when a child is headed in the wrong direction.

But training is something deeper, something that lasts. Think of an athlete going into strict training. It's not punishment—it's preparation. It's developing strength, endurance, skill, and character for what lies ahead. That's what "train up a child" really means—not just correcting bad behavior, but forming good character.

Here's the key: **study and know your children.** Their personality. Their learning style. Their interests and aptitudes. "In the way he should go" doesn't mean forcing every child down the same path. It means discovering their God-given design and training them accordingly. Whether through discipline or training, you're sowing character into them that will influence their worldview, beliefs, and values—even if for a season they turn away.

That last part of the proverb is what gives hope to weary parents: **"even when they are old, they will not turn from it."**

Recently, I shared a meal with a young man I'm mentoring who grew up as a pastor's kid. He turned away from the Lord and his family, pursuing a modern-day prodigal story—stealing, drinking, carousing—which landed him in jail on multiple occasions. Finally, he came to his senses, turned his heart back to the Lord, and reconciled with his family.

He attends a different church than his dad's now, but he's pursuing a life of faith, living by God's Word, walking in wisdom away from foolishness. **The training his parents gave him never left.** For years, it looked buried, dead, lost. But even when he was old enough to know better and still chose rebellion, that early training remained—waiting for the moment he'd come to his senses and remember the way.

I can only imagine the years of waiting for his pastor parents. The prayers. The tears. The faith required to keep believing this proverb when all evidence suggested it was a lie.

Raising kids is one of the greatest joys and most challenging assignments we're ever given in life. **It's not a formula. There are no six steps to successful parenting.** It's a life modeling faith, love, and wisdom with a whole lot of prayer.

Your role as a parent is to train them in the way they should go, trusting that even when they depart for a season, they will not ultimately turn from it.

Father, give me wisdom to train my children in the way You designed them to go—not my way, but theirs. When they depart from that path, sustain my faith through the waiting. I entrust my children to your care.

Raising Sons & Daughters

*Train up a child in the way he should go; even when
he is old, he will not depart from it.* —Proverbs 22:6

I woke up this morning with a profound thought echoing in my
mind: "My son will likely one day be raising sons!" The vision of
Grady one day fathering my grandchildren stirred something deep within me as a dad. Within moments of contemplating my future grandchildren, I found myself in prayer—praying for Grady, for his future spouse,
and even for the spouses of grandchildren yet to be born.

This morning's reading from Isaiah 48 added fuel to these prayers:
"This is what the Lord says—your Redeemer, the Holy One of Israel,
who teaches you what is best for you, who directs you in the way you
should go...if only you had paid attention to my commands,...your descendants would have been like the sand, your children like its number-
less grains; their name would never be cut off nor destroyed from before
me."

I remember a story from a few years ago, Grandma—at ninety-six
years old—spoke Psalm 71 over Grady during his second-grade biogra-
phy interview: "Even when I am old and gray, do not forsake me, my
God, till I declare your power to the next generation, your mighty acts
to all who are to come." That's a biblical vision of legacy that spans
generations. As the Spirit prompts my heart to pray, I also feel compelled
to prepare and plan for generations yet to be born. Reflecting this week,
there is one thought that resonates deeply: *stewardship of today for tomorrow.* I pray to be a faithful steward in raising my son and daughters

to have hearts that long for the Lord, who are strengthened by His Word, and who walk in His grace and love.

During a recent leadership forum, someone made an observation after reading Proverbs 3: "It's hard to seek wisdom and counsel from someone you don't know." This struck me profoundly. Let it be said of my children that they know the Lord intimately. I pray the Lord would set eternity on their hearts from an early age. I'm incredibly proud of my children today, yet I'm overwhelmed thinking about them growing up as adults with spouses and children of their own. How do I invest in them today to prepare them for tomorrow? Solomon's proverb about training up a child isn't so much a formula as it is a direction. As a father, I must act as a guide—a man being led by my Father in heaven.

The responsibility feels both humbling and inspiring. Every conversation, every discipline moment, and every prayer spoken over them contributes to their understanding of who God is and who they are as His children. My parenting becomes a reflection of how my heavenly Father parents me—with patience, wisdom, correction, and unconditional love. The generational impact cannot be overstated. The way I behave as a father today influences not just my children but potentially dozens of their descendants. When Grandma spoke that psalm over Grady, she was modeling what it means to declare God's power to the next generation. Now, it's my turn to carry that torch forward.

This isn't about perfect parenting—it's about faithful parenting. It's about being the kind of Father who points his children consistently toward their heavenly Father, creating an environment where they can develop their own authentic relationship with God.

Father, I pray for Your wisdom as we raise our children. Let me father them the way You have fathered me. Grant them hearts that hunger for You. Let them be strong in grace and power, becoming Kingdom builders who start by first building within their own families. I pray for my children's children—grant our family a legacy that enjoys You, honors You, and follows hard after You!

Rich Restraint

Do not wear yourself out to get rich; have the wisdom to show restraint. —*Proverbs 23:4*

E xhausted! I mean, I'm just completely worn out from running! One day, you're on top of the world, and then in just a moment, you're ready to give it all up. You got more than you've bargained for with your commitment. You've lost perspective. You had a vision, and the plan is nowhere in sight. You'd sell it, give it away, or pass it on to someone for a modest ask. You're ready to quit!... Have you been in this place? You may be here today!

I need to ask you a question that maybe no one has asked you before, or it's been a long time since anyone has asked you. *What drives you?* Seriously, pause, sit back, pray, and ask yourself the question: *what drives you?*

Goal-oriented leaders are driven individuals; they possess a truly inspiring energy. God has given us great strength and endurance to accomplish so many things. Yet, no man can sincerely judge his motives; it's too close. *We need the counsel of the Spirit, the Word of God, and trusted season brothers to help guide us.* Consider these words of wisdom, 'how then can anyone understand his way'? (20:24) For many men, the question *of what drives you drives you crazy!* There is much that drives us, and at times, the pressure of deadlines, bills, and commitments is immense. Consider the tensions of what drives us: driven by the approval of men instead of God, driven by fear instead of faith, driven by pride instead of humility, driven by a goal instead of a calling, driven by the allure of success in fear of failure, or a motive for money instead of the Lord. 'No one can serve two masters' (Matthew 6:24). 'For where your treasure is there, your heart will be also' (6:21). Jesus cuts to the heart of our motives, for we see what comes out of our heart by our words and actions.

The question of what drives you is not meant as a philosophical or psychological experiment. For followers of Christ, it's a daily consideration that we place before the Lord in confession and prayer whereby we ask the Lord for a renewed mind and heart that our actions may be an offering of worship in our work (Romans 12:1-2). For our work does yield a reward, and the workman is due his wage (Romans 4:4). Yet, the economy of faith yields different dividends than the world's economy.

What drives you to succeed? What *or whom are you working for?* If your drive is for success, then I want to encourage you. It's a noble task! It's a good thing you desire! Yet, success must be defined. *How do you define success in your economy?* If your bank account measures riches, then I suggest you consider a *richer* definition of success. Let's ask the rich man, 'How much is enough?' He answers, 'Only a little bit more.' His perspective will ultimately lead to exhaustion. When have you achieved success? Once defined, planned, tested, and prayed through, how will you pace yourself toward its goal? Ask God for the wisdom of restraint and the perspective of what it is to be truly rich.

With me are riches and honor, enduring wealth and prosperity (8:18). A good name is more desirable than great riches (22:1). A generous man will himself be blessed (22:9). The blessing of the Lord brings wealth (10:22). The house of the righteous contains great treasure (15:6).

Father, quiet the restless drive within me and teach me the wisdom of restraint. Help me to find my true wealth in Your presence, my purpose in Your calling, and my rest in trusting You alone.

Quiet Your Soul

Apply your heart to instruction and your ears to words of knowledge. —Proverbs 23:12

There is so much noise in our day. From the moment we wake, most people have an alarm ringing in their ears, followed by the morning news, emails, and social media messages demanding their attention. We live a life of complexity that keeps our minds and attention busy. There are meetings to attend, demands to be met, and a virtual life that never seems to end. Where is the quiet place? Where do you seek solace for your soul to listen and hear?

For it's in the quiet place that instruction and words of knowledge are waiting. For they will not pursue you only to find a deaf or busy mind fretting over the demands of the day. For it is in pursuit of instruction and knowledge that you will find them.

Consider the practical barriers to instruction and the words of knowledge. If I was to ask you, do you need wisdom? You would likely say, 'Yes, I need it for today!' How do you find wisdom? First, in the fear of the Lord. So, before we move further, prepare your heart. What do you fear? Bring to light your fears and confess them before the Lord. Let your fears be turned to measures of faith. Now, prepare your heart for instruction. For who wants to receive instruction, correction, or discipline? We must trust the Lord as a good Father who is ready to restore, renew, teach, and train for the work he has prepared for us to do today (Ephesians 2:10). My son, 8, reminds me often how hard it is to receive instruction truly. For in the moment, it does not feel very good no matter how gentle or kind its counsel is. Let us lay down our resistance by asking the question, **'How teachable am I today?'**

The old axiom is still true: *when the student is ready, the teacher will appear.* Have you prepared yourself with a teachable heart and ready for instruction? Let us be good students prepared to learn from our teacher no matter the lesson.

Words of knowledge are a refreshment and a delight to a ready soul. For those seeking answers, they find great satisfaction when their questions are resolved, their fears are alleviated, and direction is provided. These words come from the Word of God found in the scripture or a whisper from the Spirit for those attuned to hear. Words of knowledge come from family, friends, colleagues, and even the most unlikely places and people. These words of wisdom are a prophetic word of encouragement by the Spirit of God to build you up and make you strong. These words of knowledge may also come from you as well as you quiet your spirit during the noise of your day. You may receive such a word to encourage and build up a friend in need. Let the Spirit speak to you on a friend's behalf. Receive a word of encouragement and pass it along in a timely way. You may never know the gift you give for a ready soul seeking the Lord with a heart prepared for instruction. Oh, busy one! Quiet your own soul. *What is God speaking to you now?* Listen! Learn! Then, apply instruction and knowledge!

Father, quiet my heart and open my ears to receive Your instruction and the words of knowledge You desire to give me. Teach me to listen well, apply what I learn, and share Your wisdom to encourage others in their time of need.

Milestone 7: Crisis to Confirmation of My Calling

C OVID was weird. It was weird for most people, but for me, it represented a collision between confidence and crisis that I never saw coming. After navigating the career transition years before, I was hitting my stride in the work I was doing. The calling I felt like I had dialed entirely in was flourishing—we had a full pipeline, business was strong, and I felt like I was on top of the world. Then, all of a sudden in 2020, COVID hit. It was a complete shutdown—not just of society, but of my business. This truly led to a crisis at a crossroads that left me questioning everything I had invested seven years of energy into. Doubt flared up, along with familiar insecurities that I thought I had conquered.

What had I done? What was I thinking, getting into a business that was ultimately dependent on meeting in person and facilitating programs that required physical presence? All of those contracts were suddenly withdrawn overnight. What was I supposed to do now?

After months of searching, wondering, and considering my options, something began emerging in my mind that, even today, makes me wonder if it was truly of the Lord. But somehow, even in my most desperate pursuits, the Lord worked in the midst of it all. The best way I can articulate what happened is through the lens of believing that God doesn't waste anything from our lives and our stories, bringing all things together for good, no matter how difficult they may be. During that COVID season, I wondered if this was a time of integration. An entrepreneur who had run a business for fifteen years, then closed due to a financial crisis, then moved into consulting and building up leaders and teams—was this the moment to bring all these experiences together?

What happened on paper was remarkable: I launched a business, built it, ran it, and sold it all within nine months during COVID-19. On paper, you can call it a success. But what appeared successful on paper didn't quantify the crisis I felt in my soul. While everyone else was sitting at home during the shutdown, I was running harder than ever on an airplane almost every week. This led to another crisis, another crossroads in my life. In many ways, I was running scared, desperate to make a business work. An underlying question kept lingering in my mind: Is God calling me to run a business? The deeper question beneath that was: Do I have what it takes to run one?

Yet, through it all, something emerged. God's provision in allowing me to launch and then sell a business led me back to wondering about what I initially felt called to do—mentoring, coaching, and working with leaders. Had that calling truly died during this season?

Somehow, what I thought was dead was resurrected and brought back to life toward the end of COVID-19. The question that had haunted me was answered within my soul: Can I run a business? Do I have what it takes? In many ways, the answer was definitely yes.

But then came the deeper question: Is that truly God's best for me? Is that what He's called me into? Instead of running a business myself, I feel called to be a guide, mentor, and coach—a thought partner for other leaders. That's what I truly feel called to do in this season of my life.

Today, I can look back and say I'm amazed at how the Lord brought back to life what I thought had truly died. This crisis led to a confirmation of my calling. As the psalmist reminds us, the Lord brings light to dark places. Even in the darkness, you can trust Him no matter what crisis you're facing. His calling and His gifts are irrevocable (Romans 11:29)

Buy and Do Not Sell

*Buy the truth and do not sell it; get wisdom, discipline,
and understanding. —Proverbs 23:23*

Traveling to Seattle this morning before heading to my meeting, Solomon's words strike me with unusual force. For many years now, buying and selling goods has been my profession—I'm a merchant by trade. I understand the flow of commerce, the art of negotiation, and the pursuit of profitable exchanges. The better the value I provide to clients, the better the yield for everyone involved.

So when I encounter this passage in Proverbs, I'm struck by its profound wisdom. Here's a transaction that operates by entirely different rules—buy truth, wisdom, discipline, and understanding, but never sell them. This isn't about profit margins or market fluctuations; it's about acquiring assets that appreciate eternally, a concept that enlightens and inspires.

The idea of knowledge exchange has always excited me. I gain insights and share them freely with others. Yet this reminds me of my school days—cramming for tests, engaging in just-in-time learning, and watching knowledge evaporate the moment I finished writing answers. My nephew is currently preparing for the SAT and ACT, drowning in facts and formulas. How can anyone retain all that information? I shudder to think what my score would be if I took those tests today.

Ironically, while working in a profession of constant exchange for sixteen years, I'm still paying for costly mistakes that could have been avoided with better wisdom in product management and logistics. When will

I truly learn? When will I buy wisdom, discipline, and understanding in a way that transforms me permanently? When will I possess these qualities so completely that they empower and motivate me to make better decisions?

Through my work facilitating CEO peer groups, I've been studying "Business Model Generation" by Osterwalder—a comprehensive guide to strategic business planning. I'm always learning and growing, hoping to avoid future pitfalls and help others in my circle recognize similar patterns. I invest time, energy, and focus to truly own these concepts, not just rent them temporarily.

At this stage of life, I have more miles in my rearview mirror than I once did, but hopefully, many more ahead. This perspective raises crucial questions: What wisdom, discipline, and understanding do I actually own? What have I genuinely purchased along the way that has become part of my character? What insights do I need to stop treating as disposable commodities and instead weave permanently into the fabric of who I am?

The marketplace operates on quick exchanges—buy low, sell high, and maximize turnover. But Solomon's economy works differently. Some things are meant to be acquired and held forever. Truth isn't a commodity to be flipped for profit. Wisdom isn't inventory to be moved quickly. Discipline isn't a service to be outsourced. Understanding isn't a product with planned obsolescence.

These spiritual assets compound over time when held, not when traded. The person who truly 'buys' wisdom integrates it so deeply that it becomes inseparable from their decision-making process. They don't just know wise principles; they've become wise people. The same applies to discipline and understanding—they transform from external knowledge into internal character, reassuring and building confidence in their decisions.

The warning "do not sell it" suggests we'll face temptations to trade our convictions for temporary gain. Pressure to compromise our understanding for popularity. Opportunities to abandon discipline for imme-diate pleasure. Moments when selling our truth seem profitable.

But Solomon counsels us to be different kinds of merchants—acquir-ing what matters most and holding it permanently. In the commerce of daily life, let me buy what I need to keep and hold onto it until it transforms who I am.

Father, help me distinguish between knowledge that passes away and wisdom that endures. Give me the discernment to invest in truth, discipline, and understanding that will compound over a lifetime. Let these become so woven into my character that I become a man defined by wisdom rather than one who merely possesses information.

Wisdom for Hope

Know also that wisdom is sweet to your soul; if you find it, there is a future hope for you, and your hope will not be cut off. —*Proverbs 24:14*

Sitting at a Sonny's BBQ restaurant in Georgia years ago, a mentor and friend asked *what's the source of courage?* As a young man, I didn't have a good answer. I remember knowing when I had it and when I didn't. A courageous heart will face whatever hell stands in its way. A discouraged heart barely has the energy to get out the front door. You've been there. I have certainly experienced this many times in my life, on both ends of the spectrum.

Recently, I spoke with a pastor friend who is exploring vocationally what's next for him and his family. He has a pastor's heart and cares for his people, yet he's built like an engineer, project manager, and administrator. He's an incredibly gifted man. Yet, after pursuing many open doors, they've all been shut after months of diligent pursuit. It's disheartening for my friend feeling like he's coming to the end of his options. His posture today, amid heartache, is one of trust, trust that the Lord will provide and direct his steps. Have you been here? I have as well... it's a place that threatens our hope.

Your measure of hope will reveal your measure of courage. A courageous heart, who can stand against it? Yet, a heart with no hope has no courage.

When you are discouraged and find yourself with little hope, seek your solace in wisdom. What a tremendous promise 'that wisdom is sweet to your soul.' If you're filled with heartache over loss or without direction, find a place and space that's quiet in the noise of your day. Seek wisdom and the source of it. For as you see it, you will nourish your soul. In Christ, 'hope does not disappoint because God has poured out his love into our hearts by the Holy Spirit' (Romans 5:5). It's a promise regardless of how you feel; his love never fails, and hope is sustained.

If you're at a crossroads of courage and hope, then open your heart to find wisdom. 'If you find it' is conditional on your pursuit of it. God desires us to pursue Him and His promises. 'You will seek and find me when you search for me with all your heart' (Jeremiah 29:13). **Wisdom is waiting, for** wisdom's promises are found in the person of the Lord. 'If you find it' is a pursuit that starts now, this moment, asking the Lord to reveal His wisdom and ways to you. In your seeking, your hope will be restored, and your vision for the future will be renewed.

If you are dry and weary, nourish your soul today. For a weary soul has little vision beyond the day. For the hopeless makes the slow march to duty and not desire. Desire has lost its voice.

When asked even the simplest of questions, the answer surfaces, 'I don't know what I want to do.' For hope is buried deep or has gone. Find refreshment in wisdom and nurture your soul. Let hope rise in you today. Let your courageous heart be fanned to flame. You have hope and a future found in your pursuit of wisdom.

Father, fill my heart with Your wisdom so that my hope may be renewed and my courage strengthened. Guide me to seek You with all my heart, trusting that in Your ways, my future is secure and my soul refreshed.

The Righteous Will Rise

*For though a righteous man falls seven times, he rises
again, but the wicked are brought down by calamity.*
—Proverbs 24:16

L ife has its share of joys, yet it also presents challenges. Why do
the righteous fall? So they can rise again. Think of the stories that
inspire you the most. Fiction or real, we are drawn every time to the
dramas of overcoming the odds. For in the trial, when all hope seems to
be lost, courage rises. The hero of the story begins to take a stand after
falling or failing, for we cheer for the champion to increase yet again to
overcome their fears and failures. Cue the theme music; we are ready to
stand with them in their victory and celebration.

Where do you find yourself today? On the mountaintop of perspective, walking strong. If so, take time to encourage those who are weak.
If you have fallen... Grace to you! Grace to you for your moment of
struggle. For God has given grace, mercy, and forgiveness sufficient for
you today. In my circle and season, many dear friends are battling the
loss of projects, business, health, and in loss of loved ones. Grace to them
today. For they have fallen. Yet, I am confident they will rise again. They
are the righteous, not wicked, 'brought down by calamity.'

If you find yourself fallen and struggle to rise, take courage, for you are
not alone. Many have walked this road and will cheer you on as you rise
again. Take courage, for God has called you righteous as a son or daughter
of covenant. God has provided salvation for you if you reach out to him.
If you have fallen, God will provide:

- Strength to Stand – When you are weak, either by fatigue, injury, or discouragement, he will make you strong. For the Lord God is with you no matter the circumstance.

- Forgiveness when you fail – When you confess your failing, you will be cleansed and called righteous by faith in Christ. You are right before God. You are forgiven. Receive God's forgiveness today.

- Grace for loss – Loss hurts. Often, the pain is more than you can bear; grieve your loss well. Take comfort. God sees you. You have not been abandoned. He has grace for you in your loss.

In the moment, who feels like getting up again after falling? For calamity carries a weight of discouragement that dashes hope. In pain, we may be able to point to a physical trial, but what is the most significant risk for the fallen is discouragement. For one without courage, it reveals no hope. No hope reveals despair. So, to those who have fallen and your valley is so dim, lift your head. You have a Father in heaven that loves you. He has given you gifts of strength, forgiveness, and grace. Receive them. No matter how far you have fallen, rejoice! Take joy!

There is a great work happening in you (James 1:2-4, Philippians 4:4-8, Romans 5:3-5). God has given faith, peace, and love sufficient enough for you.

Father, lift me up when I fall and fill me with Your strength, grace, and forgiveness. Help me rise each time, trusting in Your righteousness and the hope You provide for every season of life.

Too Broken to Stand

For though the righteous fall seven times, they rise again. —Proverbs 24:16

I walk around with my chest out and shoulders back, head held high most of the time. That's the man I know myself to be—strong, capable, confident.

But there have been a few times in my life where I've been on the floor in a near-fetal position. So unbecoming of the man I see myself as. So crippled I could barely move, let alone stand.

If you've never been there, thank God. If you have, you know exactly what I'm talking about. That moment when life hits so hard, the floor becomes your only friend. When grief overwhelms your soul so completely that breathing feels like work. When fear grips so tightly that standing seems impossible. When hope has packed its bags and left without saying goodbye.

Have you been there? On the floor, too broken to stand?

Let me tell you what I've learned from those moments: being on the floor doesn't make you weak. It makes you human—even the righteous fall—not once, not twice, but many times. Seven is the number representing completions. The number that says "as many times as it takes."

The question isn't whether you'll fall. The question is what happens when you do.

I remember those moments vividly. The physical pain of a body racked with sobs. The emotional exhaustion of having nothing left to give. The spiritual emptiness of feeling abandoned, even though you know better. In those moments, standing feels like an act of God—because it is.

Here's what nobody tells you about rock bottom: **it's sacred ground**. The Lord meets you there, not only in the mountaintop victories, where you feel strong and capable. He's there when you're down on the floor, where you're too broken to pretend anymore.

Imagine the embrace of God the Father who loves you deeply. Picture Jesus, who sweated drops of blood in Gethsemane because He knows what it means to be crushed under impossible weight. Feel the Holy Spirit who promises to comfort and counsel you in your deepest pain.

They're all there. On the floor with you. Not standing over you with disappointment.

Not waiting for you to pull yourself together. Right there in the mess. The prophet Daniel (10:18-19) fell on his face, shaken and terrified in the presence of God's glory. An angel came and said, "Rise up." Not "Stop being weak." Not "Get it together." "Peace! Be strong now; be strong!" We too can take courage to stand firm!

That's the message today. If you're on the floor, embrace it. Let God meet you there. Feel the weight of His presence, the reality of His love. Let Him minister to your broken places.

But know this: **you won't stay there**. Though the righteous fall seven times, they rise again. There's grace for you today. Whether you fell because life knocked you down or because of something you did—grace. The Lord loves you. And at the right time, not when you feel ready but when He knows you are, you'll rise again.

Father, I'm on the floor once again. Too broken to stand. Meet me here in this mess. Let me feel Your embrace, Jesus' understanding, the Spirit's comfort. I have no strength left—but You do. When it's time, help me rise. Until then, hold me here.

Working Your Land

—◆◇◆—

Finish your outdoor work and get your fields ready;
after that, build your house. —Proverbs 24:27

The fight of a soldier and the race of an athlete inspire me deeply. These images ignite my passion, skills, and strength, stirring something powerful within my soul. Yet, for all their inspiration, they don't feed me. Paul reminds us that "the hardworking farmer should be the first to receive a share of the crops." There's wisdom in understanding the difference between what inspires us and what sustains us.

Farming is work—hard, unglamorous, patient work. I'm not afraid of it, but I recognize its demands. Preparing the land, tilling the soil, and planting seeds require discipline and focus until the job is done correctly. Then comes the waiting—for rain, for growth, for maturity, until finally harvest arrives. Harvest is glorious, but it's not constant. Most farming occurs during the mundane seasons between planting and harvesting.

Sitting in my rocker this morning, I envisioned every person in my life as a furrow in the field. Each furrow needs careful tending. Every conversation becomes a seed placed on or in the ground. The depth and value of each interaction determine how deeply that seed is planted and whether it will take root and grow. God has shown tremendous favor over the years, as well as disfavor. His favor provides direction for the way I should go, revealing which fields are ready for planting and which need more preparation.

I'm a passionate person. My fire burns bright when my vision is clear, but it quickly dims when I lose perspective in the countless details of daily business. The minutiae can overwhelm—so many details, so many moving parts. Yet today, I'm challenged to consider the fields and land the Lord has entrusted to me. What condition is this land in? What needs to be prepared, cleaned, tilled, and made ready for planting?

Here's the tension I live with: You are made to fight and run! God has prepared and empowered you for battle and competition. But you also need to eat. You must work your land so you can fight and run effectively. It's the foundation that makes everything else possible.

Solomon writes, "A wise man has great power, and a man of knowledge increases strength; for waging war you need guidance and for victory many advisors." Even in warfare, victory depends on provision and preparation. Consider the war stories of history—when supply lines were cut, advancement against the enemy ceased. No food, no water, no provision meant no victory. Yesterday, I read again about Elisha and the three kings in the Desert of Edom. God told them, "Make this valley full of ditches," and when they obeyed, "the land was filled with water."

The stories of Elijah and Elisha captivate me—the parting of waters, healing of bad water, water from ditches, and overflow of oil in the widow's pots. All reveal the miracle of blessing through provision and faithful preparation. Solomon warns us: "Like a muddied spring or polluted well is a righteous man who gives way to the wicked." When we neglect farming—the patient work of preparation and cultivation—we become unreliable sources of refreshment to others.

The lesson is clear: tend your fields first. Do the hard work of preparation. Plant seeds in relationships. Wait patiently for growth. Then, when harvest comes, you'll have the strength and resources needed for whatever battles or races lie ahead.

Father, help me embrace the patient work of farming alongside the passion for fighting and running. Show me which fields need tending, which relationships need cultivating, and which areas of my life require better preparation. Make me a reliable source of refreshment to others.

Finish Your Work In Season

Finish your outdoor work and get your fields ready;
after that, build your house.—Proverbs 24:27

I wanted to build my dream house. The vision was clear—every detail planned, every room imagined. But my fields were a mess. Unplowed. Unplanted. And I was ignoring them because the house was more exciting.

That's how I've lived too many seasons—focusing on what I wanted to build while neglecting the work that was actually in season. And it cost me. Not just productivity, but entire harvests I'll never get back.

This proverb has reprioritized my life more than once. Because here's what I kept missing: there's a season for everything, and ignoring the season doesn't make it go away. It just means you lose a year of yield.

In agricultural societies, missing harvest meant your family went hungry. Missing planting season meant no crop next year. The seasons didn't care about your preferences or your plans. They demanded wisdom and prudence—knowing what needed to happen when.

What season are you in today? Not theoretically, not eventually—right now. Are you in a season of preparation, plowing hard ground, and getting soil ready? Are you in a planting season, sowing seeds with faith that rain will come? Are you in the waiting season, trusting God for growth you can't control? Or is the harvest ripe and you need to work while the window is open?

I've made the mistake of focusing too much on building my house when I should have been working my fields. Taking vacations when harvests were rotting. Focusing on personal projects when professional work was at a critical moment. Every time, I paid for it.

The hard truth: **you can't harvest out of season, and you can't ignore the work that's in front of you without consequences.**

Your field might not be literal farmland. It could be a business that needs your attention now. A relationship that's in a critical season. A project with a deadline. A calling that won't wait. God has given you work, and there's a season when that work must be done.

Here's the promise: when you finish your outdoor work first, when you tend the fields in season, there will be a harvest. And that harvest will give you the resources—time, money, peace of mind—to build your house. But not before.

I'm learning to ask different questions. Not "What do I want to do?" but "What's in season right now?" Not "What's more fun?" but "What's required in this moment?" Not "When can I focus on me?" but "What work must I finish first?"

There's time for building your house. There's time for vacation. Time for rest. Time for Sabbath and recreation. But not when the harvest is in the field. Not when the plowing needs to happen. Not when you're ignoring the work God has given you for this season.

Father, give me wisdom to know my season. Show me what work must be finished now, in this moment, before I turn to other things. Help me resist the temptation to build my house when my fields need attention. Give me patience to work in season, faith to trust Your timing, and diligence to finish what's before me. Let the harvest come in its time.

Learned Observation

I applied my heart to what I observed and learned a lesson from what I saw. —*Proverbs 24:32*

L earning requires a discipline and focus that is not for the faint of heart. I recently watched my seven-year-old son struggle with his second-grade math homework, truly challenged by the problem and the logical deductions required to find the solution. Frustration clouded his face as he erased and rewrote his work multiple times. Yet once he discovered the formula and understood the steps needed to reach the answer, his countenance brightened immediately. Suddenly confident, he was prepared for the following problem and eager to tackle it.

The simple homework scene reveals a profound truth about how we learn and grow. Real learning happens not in the moment of easy understanding but in the struggle to grasp what initially seems beyond our reach. The breakthrough comes when we persist through the confusion and finally see the pattern, the principle, the path forward.

We can all sympathize with others going through trials or difficult seasons, even if we don't fully understand the specific details of their pain or circumstances. We recognize the universal experience of learning, growing, and maturing under the weight of challenges that seem overwhelming and may feel like they might crush us. Many of us would say after emerging from a trial, "I never want to go through that again, but I wouldn't trade what I learned through it." These challenges don't just happen to us—they shape and transform us into the people God has designed us to become, mature, and complete.

Solomon's words in Proverbs 24:32 reveal the intentionality required for authentic learning. He didn't stumble upon wisdom accidentally. He "applied his heart" to what he observed. This suggests deliberate attention, careful consideration, and purposeful reflection. Learning requires us to move beyond passive observation to active engagement with our experiences.

Consider your own life's curriculum. What lessons is God trying to teach you through your current circumstances? It may be patience through a delayed opportunity, trust through uncertain finances, forgiveness in a complex relationship, or courage in the face of an intimidating challenge. The classroom of life rarely feels comfortable, but it's remarkably effective when we apply our hearts to the lessons being taught.

The word "applied" suggests effort and intention. Just as my son had to focus his mind on the math problem, we must focus our hearts on extracting wisdom from our experiences. This means asking questions like, 'What is God revealing about Himself through this situation?' What is He revealing about me? How is He shaping my character? What patterns do I see that I need to change?

We are all shaped by the lessons of our lives, but not everyone learns from them. Some people repeat the same mistakes because they never apply their hearts to what they observe. They experience pain without gaining wisdom, go through trials without growing stronger, and face challenges without developing character. The difference between those who learn and those who endure lies in this intentional application of heart to observation. When we deliberately seek the lesson within the trial, the growth within the struggle, and the wisdom within the pain, we transform difficult experiences into invaluable education.

Father, help me to apply my heart to what I observe and learn the lessons You are teaching me through every experience. Give me discernment to see Your wisdom in the struggle and the courage to grow into the person You have designed me to be.

Good News For The Weary

Like cold water to a weary soul is good news from a distant land. —Proverbs 25:25

T he news cycle is killing us. I don't mean that metaphorically—I mean the constant drip of toxicity is literally draining life from our souls.

Doom scrolling at 11 PM. Cable news screaming at breakfast. Social media is feeding outrage all day. The spin, the negativity, the endless parade of bad news—it erodes your mind, your morale, your hope. I've watched the most optimistic people I know slowly sink into discouragement, even depression, from consuming nothing but bad news.

What are you feeding your mind? Because whatever you're consuming is shaping your soul.

Here's what I've learned: you can't control the news cycle, but you can control what you meditate on. Philippians 4:8 invites us to think about what's true, noble, right, pure, lovely, and admirable. Not as some naive denial of reality, but as a deliberate choice about where we fix our attention.

What's the good news you're dwelling on today? It could be a proverb that brought perspective. A psalm that lifted your spirit. A story that inspired you. Sometimes the best thing you can do for your well-being is let good news—real, genuine, life-giving good news—capture your thinking instead of the toxic sludge the world wants to feed you.

But here's the bigger question: **What if you became the good news for someone else?**

Think about it. There's a desert out there of people dying of thirst for something hopeful. They're drowning in bad news, surrounded by negativity, losing the fight against discouragement. And you might have exactly what they need—a word of encouragement, a story of hope, a reminder that not everything is falling apart, a testimony of what God has done to stir hope in another.

Who comes to mind? Maybe someone you've put distance between. A neighbor you haven't talked to in months—a family member you've been meaning to call. A friend from years ago who crossed your mind, but you dismissed the thought. Someone literally distant—across state or country lines—who you met once and haven't forgotten.

What if that prompting isn't random, but rather a leading from the Holy Spirit? What if they need to hear from you today?

Call them. Text them. Ask how they're doing—and actually wait for the real answer. Share something good that's happening in your life. Tell them why they matter. Offer a word of encouragement that costs you nothing but might mean everything to them.

Be like cold water to a weary soul. Be the good news from a distant land.

Because here's the truth: the best news you have isn't about politics or economics or even your personal wins. **The best news is the Good News of Jesus**—that there's hope, there's redemption, there's a future, no matter how dark today feels.

And sometimes that Good News comes wrapped in a phone call from an old friend at exactly the right moment.

Father, break me out of the news that drains my soul. Fill my mind with what's good, true, hopeful. Then make me a source of refreshment for someone dying of thirst today. Bring someone to mind who needs encouragement, and give me the courage to reach out. Let me be good news to a weary soul.

Honor, Honey, and Humility

———◆◇◆———

It is not good to eat too much honey, nor is it honorable
to seek one's honor. —*Proverbs 25:27*

'Don't believe your own press,' a businessman once said to me. Bill would never say it, but he's one of the most recognized and respected commercial real estate leaders in Atlanta. He's led an annual prayer breakfast that has been attended by thousands of leaders for years now. His credibility and reputation precede him. He's a man who's been honored. Yet, he challenged me, 'Don't believe your own press.' For pride has brought down the greatest of leaders.

Honey is sweet, yet one spoonful too much will turn your stomach. So it is with honor. It's a subtle shift from sweet to sick with even one comment that reveals the heart of the proud. We live in a culture that reflects a mantra of 'God honors those who honor themselves.' You can read only a few social media entries to validate this philosophy. Humility is a choice. *For those who are honored, we should humble ourselves before we are humbled.*

As leaders who live by wisdom, insight, and understanding in the fear of the Lord, you will be honored. 'The wise will inherit honor' (Proverbs 3:35). As you are faithful and serve with grace and integrity, your reputation will precede you. You will be honored. We must confess we all desire honor. It's a noble desire. The challenge and counsel of today's proverbs is what we will do when we are honored.

The most honorable leaders differ in honor from other contributors and then take responsibility when the results are less honorable. So, how do you guard your heart to the notoriety and accolades you receive? Graciously accept with thanks. Beware of the posture of posing behind a proud heart. It's a posture that reflects an attitude that *I'm so humble I'm proud of it.* We're all tempted toward a false humility. Again, how do you guard against such motives and temptations? It feels good, like a taste of honey that's sweet. Yet, once you taste its goodness, please share it with others who have contributed to your success. Give credit where credit is due. Celebrate others more than you're celebrated. Look for ways to honor others more than you are honored.

The higher the position of leadership, the more challenging the practice. Therefore, the higher the honor, the higher the humility should be. What's the source of humility? There are many downward slides of pride. Here's a private suggestion that may help prevent public embarrassment. Start today with a simple confession and declaration: *He is God, and I am not.*

Let that be your prayer and your posture. To humble ourselves before the Lord. Then we see He is the source of what is good and honorable in our lives. Remember the promise, 'God opposes the proud but gives grace to the humble' (Proverbs 3:35, 1 Peter 5:5). There's nothing sweeter to the soul than the grace of the humble and those who give honor to the honorable.

Father, guard my heart against pride and help me receive honor with humility, giving glory to You in all I do. Teach me to celebrate others above myself and to reflect Your grace in every place of recognition.

A Dog and His Vomit

As a dog returns to its vomit, so fools repeat their folly.—*Proverbs 26:11*

Twenty-five years of Golden Retrievers have given me irrefutable evidence of this disgusting proverb. Five different dogs. Same revolting pattern. They get sick, eat some grass, throw up, and before you can grab them, they're eating it again. Yuck!

It's nauseating. And it's exactly what Solomon is talking about.

But here's what's more disturbing: I've watched people I love do the same thing—not literally, but personally and professionally. They make a mistake, suffer the consequences, swear they've learned their lesson, then go right back and do it again. Same relationship pattern. Same financial decision. Same destructive habit. Different day, same vomit.

A CEO friend shared his interview discernment with me. He pays careful attention to candidates who claim "20 years of experience." His question: Is it truly 20 years of collective growth and learning, or is it one year of experience repeated 20 times? **The difference is massive.** One person grows, adapts, and learns from mistakes. The other keeps doing the same thing over and over, wondering why nothing changes.

My friend Kevin told me about a struggling roofing business owner in town. Every project, this guy loses money. Every single one. He underbids, underestimates costs, and runs over budget. But he keeps taking on more projects, confident he'll "make it up on volume." He's now $50,000 in the hole, running negative cash flow, and still hasn't changed his approach. **That's not a business strategy. That's a dog returning to its vomit.**

We laugh at dogs for this behavior. We think it's a disgusting animal instinct. But how many of us are doing the exact same thing with our own foolishness?

The toxic relationship you keep going back to. The spending pattern that keeps putting you in debt. The work habits that keep burning you out. The anger response that keeps destroying your relationships. The compromise that continues to cost your integrity is ongoing.

We're not dogs. We're made in the image of God. We have the capacity for wisdom, for learning, for breaking destructive cycles. But that requires honest self-examination and the humility to admit: I keep doing this, and it keeps destroying me.

Solomon doesn't mince words here. He calls it what it is: **folly.** Foolishness. The opposite of wisdom. And fools don't just make mistakes—they repeat them. Again and again, refusing to learn, refusing to change.

So here's the hard question: What's your vomit? What pattern are you repeating despite knowing it's destroying you? What lesson have you refused to learn for years—maybe decades?

Break the cycle today. Stop trading animal instincts for inspired wisdom.

Father, show me the foolish patterns I keep repeating and give me the courage to finally break them. Help me learn from my mistakes instead of returning to them —I desire years of collective wisdom, not years of repeating the same lessons.

Boasting About Tomorrow

Do not boast about tomorrow, for you do not know what a day may bring.—Proverbs 27:1

On Friday, the market dropped due to the latest political news cycle. Then on Monday, it rallies again. A CEO falls with the stock price, and layoffs soon follow. The sound investment in a house can be jeopardized when interest rates fluctuate, leaving the buyer underwater with the home value less than what they paid.

Crops planted with high hopes face drought. A new hire shows promise, only to not thrive in your workplace. Your year launches strongly, then the world shuts down with COVID, and everything you planned evaporates overnight.

We plan. We strategize. We boast about what we'll accomplish tomorrow. Then tomorrow laughs at our certainty.

James puts it even more bluntly: "Why, you do not even know what will happen tomorrow. What is your life? You are a mist that appears for a little while and then vanishes" (James 4:14). Not exactly an encouraging greeting card, but it's the truth we need to hear.

Here's what I've learned through decades of booms and busts, plans that worked and plans that crashed: **we can make our plans, yet our boast comes in the Lord to make a way.** Our trust is in Him more than our circumstances.

Health challenges come to your family, and you brace for the worst. Then you experience a miracle of healing you never saw coming. Today you're lonely, wondering if anyone cares. Tomorrow, the phone rings with exactly the encouragement you need. Grey clouds that looked permanent break with sudden rays of the sun. Broken relationships you thought were finished forever are restored with love and forgiveness you didn't know possible.

Tomorrow is a mystery—it might bring disaster or delight, and you won't know until it arrives.

The hidden gem in this proverb stands as an invitation: **be present with today rather than overly preoccupied with tomorrow.** God gives grace and peace for today. We can give Him our trust for tomorrow.

This isn't an excuse for poor planning. Make your plans. Set your goals. Work diligently. But hold them loosely, knowing "if it is the Lord's will, we will live and do this or that" (James 4:15). Our boast isn't in our certainty about tomorrow but in God's sovereignty over it.

Beware of your boast, for you never know what tomorrow will bring. The promotion you're counting on might not come. The project you're sure will succeed might fail. The relationship you think is solid might crumble. Or the opposite—the breakthrough you've stopped hoping for might arrive.

Live fully today. Plan wisely for tomorrow. But boast only in the Lord who holds both in His hands.

Father, forgive my arrogant certainty about tomorrow when I don't even control the next breath I take. Help me plan wisely but hold loosely, trusting You more than my circumstances. Give me grace for today and faith for whatever tomorrow brings—knowing You'll be there either way.

Guardrails

*The prudent see danger and take refuge, but the
simple keep going and suffer for it. —Proverbs 27:12*

I've written "Guardrails" in the margin of my Bible next to this verse, and for good reason. Life is filled with moments that test our wisdom and reveal whether we're prudent or simple in our choices. Some dangers are obvious and immediate, while others are subtle and slowly destructive.

Yesterday's trip to the fitness center pool provided a stark example of obvious temptation. Hundreds of women in revealing swimwear created a minefield for the mind and heart. The best defense in such situations is a good offense—stay focused, don't linger with your eyes, and don't allow compromising images to take root in your imagination. While I navigated the immediate situation well, later that evening, I found myself overwhelmed by the stored images and battling intense temptation. By God's grace, I maintained purity through the onslaught, but the experience reinforced how seriously we must guard our hearts and minds against anything that feeds our sinful nature.

Pool settings, with their obvious temptations, are actually easier to recognize and avoid than the more subtle dangers we face. Business dealings, for instance, present far more nuanced challenges. The promise of easy money, the pressure to cut corners, or the temptation to compromise integrity for profit—these dangers don't announce themselves with the same clarity as obvious moral temptations.

Prudence is essential. The prudent person sees danger coming and takes refuge before it's too late. They ask the hard questions: How do I need to be more wise in my decisions? How should I calculate and weigh risks? What specific dangers does this opportunity present? What's my threshold for acceptable risk versus reckless exposure? Sometimes, we must press into calculated risks as an exercise of faith, but wisdom helps us distinguish between faith-driven risks and foolish gambles. The consequences of poor judgment can be devastating—debt, broken relationships, damaged reputation, or worse. Past suffering from poor choices can cloud our judgment, making us either overly cautious or recklessly desperate to recover losses.

Solomon writes "the path of the righteous is like the morning sun, shining ever brighter till the full light of day," while "the way of the wicked is like deep darkness; they do not know what makes them stumble." The contrast is striking—clarity versus confusion, light versus darkness. The practical steps are clear: pay attention to wisdom's words, keep them always in sight, guard your heart above all else, watch your words, look straight ahead, and fix your gaze on what lies before you. Then comes the action: "Give careful thought to the paths for your feet and be steadfast in all your ways. Do not turn to the right or the left; keep your foot from evil."

The guardrails aren't meant to restrict our freedom but to protect our future. They mark the boundaries between wisdom and foolishness, between blessing and consequences. The prudent person respects boundaries, while the simple ignores them suffering the consequences.

Where do you need guardrails in your life today? What dangers do you see that require immediate refuge? What areas of compromise are slowly eroding your integrity?

Father, give me the wisdom to see danger before it's too late. Help me be prudent rather than simple, taking refuge in Your protection rather than charging ahead in my own strength. Guard my heart, guide my steps, and keep me walking steadily between the guardrails of Your wisdom.

Sharpening The Strength of Your Character

As iron sharpens iron, so one person sharpens another.—Proverbs 27:17

G rowing up in the Boy Scouts, I learned about building fires. To make a fire, you've got to have the right wood. Collecting a few sticks gives you the start, but to sustain a fire throughout the cold night, you've got to have the right fuel. At an early age, I learned quickly about chopping wood—a practice I'd carry well into my adult years, keeping fires going at home.

Here's the thing about cutting trees down or chopping wood: you'll only get so far with a dull ax or saw. It's become a timeless metaphor popularized in leadership circles—you've got to sharpen your saw. Solomon captures its essence in Ecclesiastes 10:10: "If the ax is dull and its edge unsharpened, more strength is needed, but skill will bring success."

As a boy, my Papa taught me how to use the grinder in his shop for his axes and saws. I can still smell the smoke, see the sparks flying, and notice the cinder dust on the grinder's base. I can also remember touching the blade afterward—feeling the heat even underneath my gloves.

Powerful imagery from this lesson of life, but here's what struck me: the essential ingredient for sharpening is heat. Nothing's going to change without it. True transformation comes through exposure to the grit and grind that gives you the edge you need.

Thirty years ago, I read Howard Hendricks' "As Iron Sharpens Iron," which gave a powerful reference to mentorship as the forge for character development. The idea of staying sharp inspires us, but we often lack the willingness to experience the heat.

Here's the insight that changed everything for me: **the heat comes most often in relational proximity.** In my 30-plus years of men's ministry, the number one issue I see facing men today is isolation—being disconnected from one another. Men are dulling because they're alone, working with worn-out edges, exhausting themselves trying to cut with blunt tools.

This is a challenge that requires encouragement, accountability, and living life in close proximity. It's far too easy to check out when the heat is on relationally. When conversations get uncomfortable. When someone asks hard questions. When you're exposed and vulnerable. That's when most men bail.

But **men who dare to stay connected will become sharper and more effective.** This isn't about being a jerk or using "sharp words" to cut people down. It's about being in a relationship close enough to build each other up—even when it creates friction, even when there's heat.

The sparks fly. You feel the heat. It's uncomfortable. But that's where the sharpening happens. You can't sharpen iron without friction. You can't develop character without relationships.

Who's in your life close enough to sharpen you? Who challenges you, questions you, pushes you to be better? And equally important—who are you sharpening?

Father, break through my isolation and connect me with men who will sharpen me even when it's uncomfortable. Give me the courage to stay in the heat of a real relationship instead of retreating when friction comes, knowing transformation requires both proximity and pressure.

Reflections On Your Life

As water reflects the face, so one's life reflects the heart.
—Proverbs 27:19

I thought I was hiding it well—the stress, the anxiety, the weight I was carrying. I showed up to the meeting with my game face on, ready to lead, prepared to facilitate the discussion with my client.

Then a friend asked, "You okay? You seem... well... a little on edge." With a quick, perhaps too quick reply: "No, I'm good, I'm fine."

My face betrayed me. What I thought I was concealing, my countenance was revealing. Sometimes your face doesn't lie, even when your words do.

You can see it in people's eyes—whether they're fully present or a thousand miles away. In their smile—whether it's genuine or just polite. In how they carry themselves—shoulders back with confidence or hunched under invisible weight. Even on Zoom calls, you can tell who's engaged and who's just going through the motions.

But here's what I've learned: **your face is just the surface. Your life tells the deeper truth.**

In my late twenties, I could manage my countenance in meetings. I could show up looking confident, prepared, and in control. But my calendar and bank statement told a different story. My family experienced a different version of me than the one I presented to clients and colleagues.

I thought I had the priorities in order, but my actions revealed a life out of order. Giving my best energy for clients and even at church, I then gave the leftovers to Cari and my daughters, exhausted. My life was out of order.

In my work with leaders, we facilitate 360-degree reviews where colleagues, direct reports, friends, and family weigh in on how someone shows up. It's sobering. The gap between how we think we're living and what others experience can be massive.

The review reveals not just how we look in meetings, but what we truly value by how we spend our time, money, and energy. **Your life gives you away every time.**

Here's what I've learned: most of us are terrified of that kind of vulnerability. We might manage our facial expressions, but we can't hide the patterns of our lives.

So here's a radical thought: What if you asked?

Not just "How am I coming across?" but "What does my life say I actually value?" "If you only knew me by my calendar, what would you think matters most?" "What gap do you see between what I say and how I live?"

Those are terrifying questions. In my heart, I knew something needed to change. I prayed, asking God for help, and then began conversations with Cari and a few trusted friends to find the courage to change. It prompted hard work—not just managing my activities, but examining my heart, restructuring my actual priorities, and learning to align my life with my stated values. Ultimately, in 2002, those prayerful decisions led to our move from Georgia to Colorado.

Your life reflects your heart. The question is whether you're willing to let others help you see what's being reflected and do something about it.

Father, my face can hide things temporarily, but my life reveals everything. Give me the courage to ask what my actual choices show. Help me hear the truth about the gap between my words and my life. Do the hard work in my heart so my actions reflect what You value. Make me brave enough to change not just my countenance, but my entire way of living.

Bold as a Lion

━━━━◆━━━━

The wicked man flees though no one pursues, but the righteous are as bold as a lion. —Proverbs 28:1

My heart stirs deeply with the message of boldness. The roar of a lion moves me to courageous action in the face of my fears. Thirty years ago, my wife and I were just newly married, taking a trip from Atlanta to visit friends in New York City. While we were in the city, we saw The Lion King at Radio City Music Hall. What a tear-pulling, goose-bump-giving celebration at the roar of the Lion taking his rightful place on Pride Rock. I had a similar feeling while reading and watching the Narnia stories, particularly when Aslan roars with commanding authority, bringing order and inspiring courage. For Aslan represents Christ, the Lion of Judah, in our lives. When was the last time you roared in courage and boldness?

Indeed, the expression differs from person to person, for the roar may be less from the mouth but rather a bold act that defies fear. The depth of conviction and boldness has to do with your belief.

Do you believe you are the wicked or the righteous? For the wicked hides in shame and shadows. They live under the threat of a reality that may never be realized. They are bound by fear that leads to isolation. They are disabled in their confidence. They live a life hiding in conservative corners of safety and protection of their walls of paradigms and perspectives. Their shame forces a quiet yet desperate pose in public, living under the lie that 'no one sees the real me' and 'no one cares.' Oh, dear soul, for I know this road. It's so lonely, alone while surrounded by people who genuinely love you. Yet, you cannot receive it! For guilt comes from a specific act that if we repent from the act and turn our hearts to Him, God will reconcile our sin through forgiveness, our soul will be restored, and our mind renewed. Yet, shame is far more general and deceptive. The subtlety of its lie says, 'Something must be wrong; therefore, something must be wrong with me.' For if we believe its deception, we move further into isolation and fear. I know this to be true as I see the healing tears on so many faces when the truth of love and grace from the Lord Jesus has been spoken over them. These are tears of joy as they receive the gospel of grace as if for the first time.

For in Christ, we are the righteousness of our Lord Jesus! We are called saints! Yet we sin and still walk by grace into the maturity and fullness of Christ. For by faith in Jesus, you are no longer bound by sin and shame but instead justified into his righteousness. You are clean, new, and right. Therefore, you are loved! Let me repeat it: you are loved! You are so impossibly loved by God the Father, redeemed by Christ, and empowered by the Spirit. There is also a family of Saints waiting to love and celebrate you. For when you receive this 'lavished love' (1 John 3:1), you are transformed to become a conduit of grace and a lover of people. Not hiding in shadows of shame but instead walking in the light. For these are the righteous, called and claimed by Christ. For you will know them because 'the righteous are as bold as a lion.' Let us step out of our conservative, well-constructed corners of safety. Let us believe! Let our lives reflect the righteousness of Christ in thought, words, and acts of courageous love and faith today.

Father, break the shame and fear that keep me hiding in shadows when You've declared me righteous—help me believe deeply enough to roar with the boldness of a lion. Transform me from wicked fleeing to righteous standing, from isolated hiding to courageous loving, stepping out of my safe corners into the abundant life You've called me to live.

Personal Vision

*Where there is no revelation, the people cast off
restraint but blessed is he who keeps the law.*
—Proverbs 29:18

During my early years, the King James version was the one of choice or at least the one given to me by my grandparents. In leadership circles, this verse has been frequently quoted in personal settings, in books, and at conferences. The King James is the most often quoted version, stating, 'Without a vision, the people perish.' Even yesterday at church, I prayed with a family going through some difficulty; the husband had truly lost his vision. He was so bound to the tyranny of the urgent that his actions were truly suffocating his wife and children under his pain. He lost his vision; both he and his family were dying. The principle and power of this Vision proverb is timeless.

Today, the version written above has a slightly different twist, and we should note its significance. The word 'vision' carries a depth of meaning beyond secular definitions, for the vision is a revelation from the Lord. Vision is compelling when its energy and invitation capture us. It's a dream that draws us closer, with the hope of it becoming a reality. From an organizational context, the mission is the why, and the vision is what we do. An organization without a vision will truly perish. The same is true for us. What is your vision? What are you doing today with the hope of seeing that dream be a reality tomorrow?

For the believer in Christ, it goes much deeper. Vision has to do with revelation. What has God spoken to you? How has he directed you?

When do you hear most from the Lord? Revelation is an expression of God's character and his will. Revelation has to do more with building His kingdom than our own. It has more to do with His Glory than our own. When we humble ourselves, lay down our agendas, confess our fears, and quiet our hearts, we are ready to hear from the Lord. "For the revelation awaits an appointed time" (Habakkuk 2:3.) What are we doing to prepare ourselves?

Revelation's purpose reflects what He will do and His appointed time. Yet, revelation also is the God of the universe who personally wants to reveal Himself to you. For you are holy and set apart by God for a relationship with Him. He invites you to be with Him (Revelation 3:20) to experience life together to the full, for it's in His presence that He will reveal Himself to you by His Spirit and through His promises. He wants to reveal Himself to you so you will be changed, sanctified, and transformed. It's in these sacred moments of His presence that He reveals a vision of revelation to you. These moments are when you find life, purpose, and direction. For the God of the universe has spoken vision and revelation to you. There is nothing more fulfilling and satisfying to the soul. For you are and will be 'blessed' as you keep His promises.

Father, open my heart to receive Your revelation and give me clarity to walk in the vision You have for my life. Help me to trust Your timing, keep Your ways, and allow Your Spirit to guide every step toward the fulfillment of Your purposes.

You're Not Enough

———◆○◆———

Fear of man will prove to be a snare, but whoever
trusts in the Lord is kept safe. —Proverbs 29:25

S ome lies get spoken over you so early, so often, that you stop recognizing them as lies. They become your truth. Your reality. A snare
that's got a hold on you.

As a young man, words were spoken over me that took root deep in
my soul: "You're not smart enough. You're not capable enough. You can't
follow through." These weren't just casual criticisms—they were curses
that shaped how I saw myself for decades.

I believed them. Every single word. And the stress of that belief nearly
killed me.

Physically symptoms though the stress nearly caused a heart attack
that put me in the cardiologist office. Later I realized the spiritual, mental, and emotional effects of these lies created a performance treadmill I
couldn't escape. If I could work harder, achieve more, prove myself again
and again, maybe then I'd finally be enough.

The trap of performance is exhausting. You're never done. There's
always another mountain to climb, another goal to hit, another person
to impress. You run faster, work longer, push harder—all to silence that
voice saying you're not enough.

I performed my way through my twenties, my thirties, even into my
forties. Every success was a temporary relief. Every setback was confirmation of what I'd always feared: maybe they were right. Perhaps I wasn't
smart enough, capable enough, or good enough.

At its core I battled my fear of man's opinion and their approval became my master. What would people think if I failed? What would they say if I admitted I was struggling? The snare of needing approval, acceptance, validation—it wrapped tighter around my throat every year.

Then one day, in complete exhaustion and exasperation, *grace invaded my soul*.

I can't point to a specific moment or dramatic event. It was more like finally letting go after holding your breath for thirty years. The dream of just being good enough for who I was—not who I needed to become, not who others expected me to be—but just me. As I am. With all my limitations and failures.

What an incredible invitation: to stop performing, to stop running, to stop trying to earn what's already been freely given. The lie that ran me to the ground was this: "You have to prove you're enough." The truth that saved me was this: "Even with all my shortcomings, failures, and weakness, I am enough in the love and grace of Christ."

Not because I had finally achieved enough, or become smart enough, or proved capable enough. But because the Lord says so. Period. His grace provides safety for souls worn out from performance. His acceptance isn't based on achievement.

Maybe a parent spoke lies over you. Maybe a coach, mentor, friend, or even a pastor. Perhaps you've spent decades running from those words, trying to prove them wrong through sheer force of will and endless effort.

Let me tell you: **you can't outrun a lie. You can only replace it with a grace-filled truth.**

The truth is this—you don't have to perform for God's approval. You don't have to earn His love. You don't have to prove your worth. The fear of man is a snare, but trust in the Lord brings safety. Real safety. Soul-deep safety.

Stop running. Stop performing. Let go of the expectation to meet some standard that was never meant for you to carry. Find refuge in the only One whose opinion actually matters.

Father, I'm tired of running. Tired of performing. Tired of trying to prove I'm enough. The lies spoken over me have held me captive too long. Today, I choose to trust You instead of fearing man. Let Your grace be louder than every lie. Let your acceptance be deeper than every rejection. Keep me safe in You.

Noble Wife

A wife of noble character who can find? She is worth far more than rubies. —Proverbs 31:10

Celebration of my wife is one of the greatest joys I have in life. Celebrations in everyday moments, such as sharing a morning coffee, midday lunch dates, a quick walk around the loop on a warm day, and evening prayers before we say goodnight. In 30 plus years of marriage, we have had hundreds, even thousands of moments of celebration that warm my heart. There are a few grand memories of vacations and anniversaries that are fun to remember. Yet, I find so much joy in the day-to-day moments to cherish my wife. Yet, I'm mindful of the times of neglect as well when the demands of life or my ambitions have distracted me from what matters most.

Jesus says, 'For where your treasure is, there your heart will be also' (Matthew 6:21.) His words cut to the heart of our motives and values. We only have to look at our calendars and checkbooks to see what we value by how we spend our time and money.

Jesus calls us to build His Kingdom through the hearts of people turning towards Him. The ultimate treasure is found in the hearts of people, not in the riches of this world. However, our focus often gets a little skewed as we work for riches to give to those we love. Then, in our pursuit of riches, we neglect the very object of our love. It's a daily battle for our attention and hearts to be renewed in what matters most, beginning with our families. As I heard recently in a movie clip, 'Your kids will grow and leave home; it's your spouse who will remain.' *What are you doing to treasure your most precious relationship?*

Read and reflect through Proverbs 31. 'Who can find' such a woman? The woman I read about in this passage is honored, cherished, and loved. She is celebrated as a woman of great value and worth. Indeed, 'she is worth far more than rubies.' In this moment of reading and reflection, *beware of comparison.* Rid yourself of that root that will only emphasize your discontentment. Whether you are married or single, instead of contrast, consider a vision of your wife! For you have a wife of nobility today. Christ has spoken that over her as a daughter of the King. Every day, she takes another step toward realizing her vision. She steps further into the reality of who Christ says she is in His eyes. She is a treasure, one worthy of great value. So, beware of neglect in pursuit of other riches and missing the most incredible gift and treasure in the woman you love. Pray and ask God to give you a vision for your wife. Cherish her today by speaking about the value, worth, and truth of God's nobility over her at every opportunity.

Who can find a wife of noble character? To the married men... You already have her; cherish her with your thoughts, words, and actions today. Speak vision and a future over her. Echo the promises of God by washing her in the word (Ephesians 5:26.) Love and pursue her more than the value of riches. 'Who can find her?'...Let us not neglect her. No matter the health of your marriage, take one step towards her, stay steady, and continue your pursuit today and for the rest of your days, for the blessing of her beauty and nobility awaits.

Father, help me to cherish and honor the noble wife You have given me, seeing her worth through Your eyes and not the world's. Grant me the wisdom and heart to celebrate, love, and serve her daily, reflecting Your love in every word and action.

Milestone 8: Finish What's Been Started

———◆◯◆———

I'm not quite on my last lap, but I am in my fifties, and I see things through the perspective of what it looks like to finish well. It is a season where many of my mentors—now in their seventies and eighties—are on their homeward journey, heading toward Heaven. Watching them finish well has cast a vision and created an opportunity for me to consider what it means to finish well myself.

In this season, even as a marker and milestone for this book, Wisdom on the Way represents something deeply personal about stewardship and faithfulness. This manuscript was written 12 years ago, and for whatever reason laid dormant for nearly a decade. The project that was originally written during my crisis career, is now being completed as an act of faith—an example of finishing what's been started.

That's my challenge for you as we close this journey together: What is the thing that God has called you to do that He is inviting you to trust Him with? What is He asking you to lean into through small steps of faith, following the Lord's direction for your life one step at a time in the pursuit of wisdom?

What is that thing you have started that He's called you to finish?

In many ways, it's just like the ascent of a mountain summit you might imagine as you consider your milestones along the way. The trails before us are looking toward a summit that appears daunting—how will we ever be able to ascend to that level of height? The answer, in many ways, is simple: one step at a time toward reaching that goal at the summit.

The goal of finishing what you started is often achieved simply by being faithful to the milestones and each day that lies ahead. Just as I've tried to demonstrate throughout each of these milestone moments, being faithful to pursue wisdom every day will help you move further along the path.

Sometimes, the things we're called to finish don't look like grand gestures or dramatic transformations. Sometimes, they're as simple as a manuscript that sat in a drawer for a decade, waiting for the right moment to be shared. Sometimes, they're the daily disciplines of loving our families well, serving in our communities, or stewarding the gifts and calling God has placed on our lives.

The beauty of each milestone is that it's not an ending—it's a continuation. It's a recognition that the pursuit of wisdom is a lifelong journey, and finishing well means staying faithful to that pursuit regardless of the season we find ourselves in.

As I've learned through each of these milestones—from that transformative summer at fourteen, through marriage, entrepreneurship, fatherhood, major moves, career transitions, and seasons of crisis—the common thread has always been the pursuit of wisdom and God's faithfulness to guide each step.

As we conclude this journey together, remember that wisdom is always available. God is a generous giver, and He will give wisdom to all who ask and seek it. He will provide it and guide you in the way of wisdom.

Wisdom on the Way - Topical Summary Guide

30 Essential Topics for Life Guidance

8 Milestone Moments

Quick Reference by Life Situation:

WHEN YOU'RE STRUGGLING - 11, 180, 190, 193, 202
   WHEN YOU NEED DIRECTION - 19, 24, 127, 172
   WHEN FACING TEMPTATION - 36, 47, 184, 188
   WHEN IN CONFLICT - 63, 125, 208, 211
   WHEN YOU NEED ENCOURAGEMENT - 114, 153, 156, 202
   WHEN MAKING DECISIONS - 101, 106, 111, 130

Acknowledgments

*W*isdom on the Way was written during my darkest days of career change and financial crisis while caring for my family, stepping out into the unknown, and "trusting the Lord to direct my steps" (Proverbs 3:5-6). These pages reflect the wisdom of those who marked my life and modeled a life in pursuit of it. I am deeply grateful for their influence and guidance.

First, my Dad, Jim Verhey, who has since gone to be with the Lord, invested a season in meeting over pancakes to discuss Proverbs, reading from his old blue King James Bible. This was followed by hundreds of conversations that reminded me, "what works works" when trusting the Lord. To his dad, my Papa, who even after his stroke continually reminded me to "number our days aright, that we may gain a heart of wisdom" (Psalm 90:12). Papa, even in his nineties, reminded me to read the Word like it's a letter from your Father. To Grandma, who spent years in the garden tending this young man's heart in God's Word and in life. Dad, Papa, and Grandma—I miss you all.

To Mom and Steve, for sharing the wisdom of your life, enjoying the fullness of each day, love of family, resilience during hard times, and the wisdom of travel to never stop exploring. To Mom and Dad Regehr, you continue to show love, support, and prayers to be a man, husband, father, and workman in pursuit of wisdom. To Aunt Pat and Uncle Bob, a lifetime of faithfulness for more than fifty years in service, leading kids to Christ at camp, and many more years in pursuit of His Word and wisdom on the way. I am the fruit of your life, sowing God's Word in my heart. To Uncle Dan, how many miles you've hiked the Appalachian Trail, sowing a love for the outdoors in my life, letting the trail be a metaphor for life, and your faithfulness as a writer of trail guides and biblical guides to the testimony of God's ways and wisdom.

To William, my brother, your quiet strength, faith, resilience, and way with words have encouraged me over the years. To Scott and Deb, your friendship, partnership in ministry, love, and continuous support meant more than you know during my darker days. To the men and mentors who've continuously spurred me on in friendship, strength, and love: Paul and Phyllis Stanley, Dave Jewitt, Gary Klinger, Tom Grady, Sam Voorhies, Michael Brunner, Peter Jackson, Fabian and Kathrin Heinze, Jason Foster, Ed Behr, my Convene CEO team, Friday Mission Men, New Life Church pastors and family, Young Adults community and homegroup, all my 14er hiking buddies, and my coaching clients since 2012.

My greatest acknowledgment goes to my sweetheart, Cari, love of my life and best friend, for your devotion and encouragement to trust the Lord with all my heart. To my children, Ellie, Bethany, Matthias, and Grady—you have my heart and my devotion to be a man of wisdom to father you well.

Whatever I have regarding wisdom only comes from the Lord. He is my Father, Savior, and Counselor. Wisdom is a free commodity if only pursued as a gift from the Lord. If you don't know this relationship with Him, I invite you to turn your heart to the Lord. He will meet you wherever you are on the journey.

About the Author

R ussell Verhey is a leadership mentor, coach, and workplace psychologist with deep roots in entrepreneurship.

Since 2002, Russell has been based in Colorado Springs. He has built a multifaceted career focused on leadership development. Since 2012, he facilitates CEO peer groups, provides executive coaching, and has taught as an adjunct professor at UCCS and OD Consultant at UCHealth for several years. As a consultant, Russell has worked with Fortune-level companies to design leadership programs, mentor executives, and reshape organizational cultures. His approach emphasizes positivity and measurable outcomes in employee well-being, productivity, and retention.

Russell's credentials include a master's in leadership from Denver Seminary and a Ph.D. in Industrial-Organizational Psychology. He's an ICF MCC coach with multiple coaching certifications and is a member of several professional organizations. In 2016, Russell authored "The Conversationalist," exploring relationship-building through meaningful dialogue. Then, published his dissertation work in "Spiraling Up", a leader's response to negativity in the workplace.

Family and faith are central to Russell's life and work. For 15 years, he and his family organized father-child retreats to foster deeper connections. He takes pride in his 30+ year marriage to Cari and their children. An avid outdoors person, Russell enjoys exploring new places, fresh powder skiing, endurance races, and summiting the 58 Colorado fourteeners. He's a decade-long veteran of the 15-minute power nap during the workday and enjoys taking long walks to unwind with his Golden Retriever "grand-puppy" Winston.

Dr. Russell Verhey's diverse background, spanning construction, entrepreneurship, organization, and leadership development, uniquely informs his work. His goal is to inspire positive change in leaders and organizations through thoughtful coaching, mentoring, and facilitation. Dr. Verhey's warm personality and 'contagious optimism' have made him a sought-after guide for leaders navigating complex challenges.

Feel free to Connect with Russell on LinkedIn

For speaking, consulting, or coaching contact him directly at russell @leadersadvance.net

For more regular writing updates from Russell subscribe to Advance Leadership Insights

www.ingramcontent.com/pod-product-compliance
Lightning Source LLC
Chambersburg PA
CBHW051956090426
42741CB00008B/1412